P9-DFL-334

Psychology

by
Theo Sonderegger, Ph.D.

Cliffs Notes

INCORPORATED

LINCOLN, NEBRASKA 68501

Cliffs Quick Review Psychology

Acknowledgments

My sincere thanks go to Michele Spence of Cliffs Notes for her excellent editorial assistance, tactfulness, infinite patience, and general help in the preparation of this book. Thanks, too, to my family for their encouragement and support. I deeply appreciate the help of my colleagues and former students who unfailingly provided up-to-date information from many areas of psychology concerning the current status of controversial issues in the ever-changing and fascinating study of human behavior.

Cover photograph by Michel Tcherevkoff, Ltd./The Image Bank

FIRST EDITION

CONTENTS

CONTENTS

CONTENTS

CONTENTS

CONTENTS

CONTENTS

CONTENTS

CONTENTS

CONTENTS

CONTENTS

APPENDIX

A science can be thought of as an **organized body of knowledge gained through application of scientific methods.** An understanding of a particular science allows a scientist to predict and to control events within it.

Psychology is the **science of behavior and mental processes.** As human beings, we are all practicing psychologists, seeking to understand and predict our own behavior and, as the need arises, the behavior of others. But while we all experience some success in that endeavor, most of us are unaware of the complexity of psychological processes.

A good analogy compares a living being's mental process to a computer's functioning. Both person and computer need

- input from the environment
- internal processing
- memory storage
- output

But a computer would have to be as large as a football field and use technology that currently doesn't exist to rival the human brain. To understand behavior and mental processes, that is, to understand psychology, one must study the mechanisms (the procedures) for

- environmental input to the organism
- receiving the input
- processing the information
- storing the information
- accessing the information
- converting the information into action

A Brief History of Psychology

The content areas of psychology and the techniques for studying them have prompted extensive debate because views of how the mind functions differ. In the 1800s, both physiologists and philosophers investigated that functioning from the perspective of their disciplines, but it wasn't until 1879 that Wilhelm Wundt (1832–1920) established the first research laboratory (at the University of Leipzig) for the study of psychology per se—an event that marks the birth of psychology as a science.

Early Views of Psychology

Structuralism. **Structuralists** consider the subject matter of psychology to be human consciousness and suggest that consciousness be analyzed in terms of sensations and feelings (which, when organized, form the structure of the mind). Edward Titchener (1867–1927) a well-known structuralist, founded a psychology laboratory at Cornell University. To obtain data, structuralists use a technique called **introspection,** the process of examining what is happening in one's mind and what one is thinking and feeling.

Functionalism. **Functionalists** propose that dynamic functions, rather than structural components, of the mind constitute the nature of psychology and stress adaptation to the environment. William James (1842–1910), an American psychologist, published the landmark functionalist text *Principles of Psychology* in 1890. John Dewey, another American (psychologist, philosopher, and educator), argued that psychology should deal with how people adjust to their environment.

Gestalt psychology. **Gestalt psychology,** like functionalism, discounts structure in describing the functioning of the human mind. It focuses instead on the totality of a perception. Max Wertheimer (1880–1943) contended that understanding of conscious experience does not rely on breaking the experience into its components. For example, to enjoy music at a concert, we don't have to know the qualifications of each member of the orchestra, the quality of their instruments, how the performers are dressed, the extent of the conductor's training, and so forth to enjoy the performance as a whole.

Behaviorism. **Behaviorism** emerged partially as a reaction against functionalism. John Watson (1878–1958) argued that the behavior of animals can be more accurately described in terms of simple acts, or behaviors, rather than in terms of intent. The work of Russian physiologist Ivan Pavlov (1849–1936) presented evidence, for example, of how the sound of a bell can elicit a response such as salivation in a dog. From the behaviorists' work arose the idea that psychology should primarily study only **observable behavior.**

Psychoanalysis. Sigmund Freud (1856–1939), a Viennese neurologist, developed a highly successful approach to treating people with emotional and mental problems, many of them women who exhibited problems with physical functioning that had no clear underlying physical causes. Freud proposed that the dysfunctions, given the diagnosis of **hysteria,** were based on unconscious conflicts. The process of raising these conflicts to a level of awareness became known as **psychoanalysis.** Because Victorian society severely restricted and regulated the behavior of women, it is understandable that many of the problems involved sexual matters and that psychoanalysis addresses, among other things, the development of the sexually mature person.

Current Views of Psychology

Contemporary psychologists, rather than debating the nature of psychology or the human mind, focus on understanding human functioning.

Humanistic views. **Humanistic views** stress the uniqueness of the individual, contend that individuals use **free will** in determining their future, and suggest that the desire for **self-actualization,** the fulfillment of human potential, is the prime motivation of life. Psychologist Carl Rogers (1902–87) is associated with the humanistic approach to psychotherapy, which he termed **client-centered therapy.**

Cognitive views. **Cognitive views,** which developed partially in response to behaviorism, contend that mental (symbolic) processes (learning, memory, thinking, and perception) as well as physiological responses must be considered in understanding behavior.

Neurobiological views. **Neurobiological views** emphasize biological and neurological bases as essential underpinnings of behavior and mental processes. Proponents of this view are interested in, in addition to the effects of heredity and environment on behavior, how the central nervous system and its components (both structural and chemical) affect physiological processes. For example, current research investigates how drugs (both medicinal and recreational) affect the central nervous system and development of the organism and how effects of such drugs might possibly be transmitted from parents to offspring.

Learning/behavioral views. Those who favor **learning/behavioral views** focus on strategies to investigate the effects of experience and other factors on behavior. Investigations based on this perspective may be carried out in the clinic as well as in the laboratory.

Psychodynamic views. Psychodynamic views, seen in some approaches to personality theory or strategies for psychotherapy, stress the important effect of early experiences, often in unconscious processes, on later behavior.

Sociocultural views. Some believe that **sociocultural factors** (that is, factors involving a combination of social and cultural elements) such as the effects of gender, ethnicity, culture, and social status affect behavior and must be evaluated in order to understand and predict it. Interest in such factors has led to the development of many new areas in psychology, such as ethnic studies and the psychology of gender.

Major Fields in Psychology

Many modern subdisciplines in psychology have resulted from the array of approaches used to study behavior and mental processes. The American Psychological Association (1995) listed 42 Divisions (representing different areas of psychology) and a total membership of 82,664. Many jobs requiring knowledge in these subdisciplines are in university settings. Major fields in psychology include the following (percentages of psychologists working in each area are listed in parentheses).

Providers in psychological fields.

- **Child clinical psychologists** (1.5%) assess problems of children and provide psychotherapy to help resolve the problems.

- **Clinical psychologists** (42.4%) assess clients' problems in daily functioning and provide psychotherapy to help resolve behavior problems.

- **Counseling psychologists** (10.1%) help people resolve problems in daily living (usually problems less severe than those of the people seen by clinical psychologists).

- **Geropsychologists** (0.2%) provide services for the older population.

- **Health psychologists** (0.9%) work to determine how health—including, for example, the effect of lifestyles upon it—affects functioning.

- **School psychologists** (3.9%) work with children, parents, and teachers to accomplish educational goals.

Research and other psychology fields.

- **Cognitive psychologists** (0.7%) are concerned with thought processes (relationships between memory, learning, and perception).

- **Developmental psychologists** (4%) study the physical, emotional, cognitive, and social changes occurring over the life span.

- **Educational psychologists** (2.3%) work to facilitate/maximize learning in the classroom.

- **Experimental psychologists** (1.7%) focus on research methodology and try to identify and focus on the basic elements of behavior and mental processes.

- **Industrial/organizational psychologists** (3.6%) deal with the relationships between people and work and also may study the behavior of people in organizations.

- **Personality psychologists** (5%) are interested in individual differences as expressed in the traits and characteristics exhibited by the individual.

- **Physiological/psychobiological psychologists** (0.5%) study brain, biology, and behavior relationships.

- **Psychopharmacology psychologists** (0.2%) are interested in the effects of psychopharmacological agents (and other drugs) upon behavior.

- **Quantitative/mathematical/psychometric/statistical psychologists** (0.5 %) are interested in developing and applying mathematical procedures for psychological research.

- **Social psychologists** (2.4%) are interested in the effects of social situations and cultures upon an individual's behavior.

The remainder of psychologists apply their psychological information to work in other disciplines. For example, law psychology majors may have degrees in law or legal studies as well as in psychology and are interested in legal situation behaviors (for example, jury selection). Sports psychologists are concerned with motivating and training athletes and with the effects of exercise on lifestyles. Engineering psychologists, sometimes known as human-factor psychologists, deal with the use of psychological theory in managing work (for example, skill in handling machines).

Psychology is, as is any science, a branch of knowledge that deals with a body of facts systematically arranged and shows the operation of general laws.

The Scientific Method

In all sciences, including psychology, a special procedure, the **scientific method,** must be used to collect data to answer a question or to solve a problem. The scientific method not only answers the question at hand but also is used to construct scientific **theories.** A **theory** is systematically organized knowledge applicable in a wide variety of circumstances. (The amount of information available in any science is too vast to be useful unless it is organized through the use of theories.) Theories are also used to predict events or to answer questions in a specific scientific discipline. In psychology, theories are used to organize and predict behavior and mental processes. The findings of a particular study may support or lead to the alteration of a theory.

While the scientific method doesn't provide a step-by-step recipe for dealing with specific circumstances, it does provide general guidelines for the following procedures in any scientific data collection.

- formulation of the problem
- design of the study
- collection of data
- analysis of data
- conclusions drawn from data

The description of a study, its procedures, and its conclusions is frequently published as an article in a scientific journal. Careful attention to following the scientific method allows a second investigator to **replicate** or **refute** the findings of a study. For ease of replication, the variables (items under consideration in a study that can change or vary during the course of the study) in a study are defined in terms of *observable* operations called **operational definitions.**

Descriptive/Correlational Research

Any scientific process begins with **description,** based on observation, of an event or events, from which theories may later be developed to explain the observations. In psychology, techniques used to describe behavior include case studies, surveys, naturalistic observation, interviews, and psychological tests.

Case studies. A **case study** is a method of obtaining information from the detailed observation of an individual or individuals. Much information about behavior and mental processes has been obtained through such studies of individual clinical cases. (Sigmund Freud, for example, formulated psychoanalytic theory after many years of treating and studying patients with emotional problems.) Although valuable information about certain types of problems may be obtained by this method, the procedure is time consuming, and it is difficult to obtain data from a broad sampling of people.

Surveys. In a **survey,** people from a wide sample are asked questions about the topic of concern. The Kinsey survey on sexual behavior is a well-known example. Surveys can supply useful information, but they have their problems and limitations. For example, the people who respond may not be representative of the population in general, or those polled may be reluctant to respond to questionnaires or to answer them accurately.

Naturalistic observation. In another approach to gathering information, **naturalistic observation,** people or animals are observed in their everyday behaviors, and their behaviors of interest are documented. For example, valuable information on wild animals, such as lions, has come from studying them in their natural habitats as opposed to observing them in a zoo because their zoo behavior may be quite different from their natural behavior. Similarly, the behavior of a human in a home environment may differ considerably from that in a laboratory.

Psychological testing. Many standardized procedures **(tests)** have been developed to measure specific behaviors or characteristics of organisms. Most of us have been subjected to such tests—for example, the intelligence, aptitude, and achievement tests used to predict behaviors. To be useful, tests must be both **reliable** and **valid** (see p. 165).

Correlation. **Correlation,** a statistical measure of a relationship between two or more variables, gives an indication of how one variable may predict another. The descriptive techniques discussed above permit a statement, in the form of correlations, about that relationship. However, *correlation does not imply causation;* that is, simply because two events are in some way correlated (related) does not mean that one necessarily causes the other. For example, some test data indicate that boys receive higher math-aptitude scores on college entrance exams than girls, indicating a correlation of gender with mathematical ability. But before concluding that gender *determines* mathematics aptitude, one must demonstrate that both the boys and the girls in the study have had the same mathematics background. Some studies have shown that girls are discouraged from taking or at least not encouraged to take more than the minimum mathematics requirements. Such discrepancies in mathematical accomplishment may also arise in the home—for example, from a parental belief that a girl does not need much mathematical training to be a good wife and mother.

Experimental Research

If researchers intend to make cause-and-effect statements, they typically use **experimental research,** which is usually, but not always, conducted in a laboratory. The laboratory environment allows the experimenter to make controlled observations using the steps of the scientific method.

Formulation of the problem. In formulating the problem in a psychological study, the researcher raises a question about behavior or mental processes. Perhaps the investigator wonders whether certain environmental conditions improve or adversely affect motor performance. The investigator might operationally define the environmental condition of interest as "background music" and the motor performance as "typing speed." Next, the investigator proposes an answer to the research question ("What is the relationship between typing speed and background noise?), an answer called a hypothesis. A **hypothesis** postulates a relationship between two variables, an **independent variable** (that which the experimenter manipulates—in this case, the background music) and a **dependent variable** (that which changes as a consequence of manipulation of the independent variable—in this case, the typing speed). The experimenter hypothesizes that "an increase in loudness of background music will produce a decrease in typing speed."

Design of the study. Once the problem to be investigated has been selected, the experimenter must decide how to conduct the study. Much of the information used in psychology and other sciences has been collected in laboratory situations because they facilitate the use of many controls during data collection. In the background music/ typing speed study, for example, all subjects would be taken to a laboratory for testing and would use the same typewriters to take the typing tests. The experimenter would have to decide whether to use two groups of subjects with comparable typing skills and expose one group to a music loudness level different from that used with the other (a **between-subjects design**) or sequentially expose the same subjects to music of two loudness levels (a **within-subjects design**). Each procedure has advantages and disadvantages. (Decisions concerning the procedure to use depend on many factors, which are studied in experimental design courses.)

Collection of data. The experimenter collects data (typing speed at different loudness levels) to test the hypothesis according to the selected experimental design.

Analysis of data. The data are analyzed by appropriate statistical methods (see the Appendix, p. 193). In this case, mean scores of the two sets of typing speed/loudness level data would be compared to see if differences are significant or could be due to chance.

Conclusions drawn from the data. Based on analysis of data, conclusions may be drawn about the hypothesized relationship between the independent and dependent variables. The hypothesis, that "an increase in loudness of background music will produce a decrease in typing speed," may be supported by the data (the increase in loudness of background music—manipulation of the independent variable—*did* produce a decrease in typing speed—the dependent variable) or may not be supported by the data (the increase in loudness *did not* produce a decrease in typing speed).

Reporting results. The process used in and the results obtained from the study are gathered and written. If the study results are of sufficient significance, they may be published in a scientific journal (as mentioned above, allowing the study to be replicated or refuted by another researcher) and may eventually be used quite pragmatically. For example, if a study determines that background music (or perhaps background music of a certain loudness level) improves typing performance, certain employers would be likely to make use of the findings in their businesses. Scientific knowledge in all sciences grows as a result of information collected through the scientific method.

Basic and applied research. The goal of **basic research** in psychology is primarily to describe and understand behavior and mental processes without immediate concern for a practical use. Such research, usually conducted in university settings, is essential to the expansion of scientific knowledge and the development of theories. **Applied research** uses scientific studies to solve problems of everyday life.

In reality, there is crossover between the two types of research. For example, after conducting basic science experiments to delineate the neural mechanisms associated with Parkinson's disease, the same researcher might then undertake an applied project by continuing the study to find a therapeutic drug that alters the functioning of identified neural mechanisms of the disorder and thereby relieves the symptoms.

Ethical Considerations

Ethical considerations are taken into account when an experiment is planned. In most academic institutions, the proposed experimental protocol is reviewed by an institutional review board to ensure that experimental procedures are appropriate (if they are not, federal funds will not be granted for the research). In dealing with human subjects, psychologists follow a code of ethical principles published by the American Psychological Association, which requires investigators to

- obtain informed consent from all subjects
- protect subjects from harm and discomfort
- treat all experimental data confidentially
- explain the experiment and the results to the subjects afterward

Similarly, when research is conducted with animals, the project is reviewed by an institutional animal care and use committee (IACUC) to be certain that it is necessary to use animals as subjects to test the hypotheses and that other procedures are not feasible. It also determines that appropriate sample sizes and procedures are used in the experiment and that animals will be given proper care. The IACUC also periodically visits all of the animal colonies to ensure that the research animals are appropriately cared for.

Behavior and mental processes result from activities in the body's nervous system and other physiological systems. (Using the comparison made earlier, the nervous system is analogous to computer hardware.)

Neurons

Structure. The basic unit of the nervous system is a cell known as the **neuron** (Figure 1). It is estimated that the nervous system contains over 11 billion neurons. The neuron, which is covered by a **cell membrane,** consists of

- **dendrites,** branched appendages that carry information to the cell body

- a **cell body (soma),** which contains the nucleus

- an **axon,** which conveys information away from the cell body

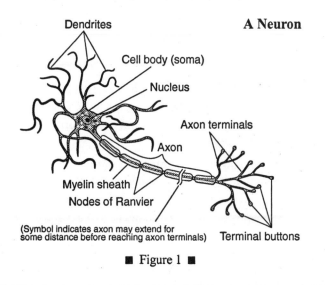

A Neuron

(Symbol indicates axon may extend for some distance before reaching axon terminals)

■ Figure 1 ■

Some axons are covered with a **myelin sheath** (interspersed with spaces called **nodes of Ranvier**), which aids in neural transmission. Neurons are surrounded by **glial** cells, which nourish the neurons and hold them in place; these cells are the basis of the myelin sheaths. **Axon terminals** are branched and contain **terminal buttons,** tiny swellings that in turn contain **synaptic vesicles** (Figure 2). Synaptic vesicles are filled with chemicals called **neurotransmitters,** which assist in transmission of information to other neurons.

A Synapse

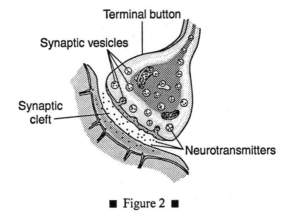

■ Figure 2 ■

Types of neurons. There are three types of neurons:

- **Sensory neurons** are located in the body's sense organs (for example, the eye, ear, or nose) and send information from these organs to the brain.

- **Motor neurons** convey information from the nervous system to the body's organs, glands, and muscles.

- **Interneurons** (association neurons) transmit information from one neuron to another within the nervous system.

Neural Transmission

The function of a neuron is to transmit information within the nervous system. **Neural transmission** occurs when a neuron is activated, or fired (sends out an electrical impulse). Activation (firing) of the neuron takes place when the neuron is stimulated by pressure, heat, light, or chemical information from other cells. (The type of stimulation necessary to produce firing depends on the type of neuron.) The fluid inside a neuron is separated from that outside by a polarized cell membrane that contains electrically charged particles known as ions. When a neuron is sufficiently stimulated to reach the **neural threshold** (a level of stimulation below which the cell does not fire), **depolarization,** or a change in cell potential, occurs.

Potentials. The term **potential** refers to a difference in electrical charges. Neurons have two types of potentials, a resting potential and an action potential. The neural threshold must be reached before a change from resting to action potential occurs (Figure 3).

Transmission of a Nerve Impulse

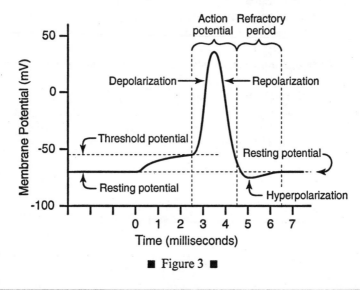

■ Figure 3 ■

Resting potential is the potential maintained by the inactive neuron. When unstimulated, a neuron is like a small battery and has a measurable negative electrical charge (about 70 millivolts) called the resting potential.

Action potential is the potential produced when appropriate stimulation is high enough to reach the neural threshold and causes the neuron to **fire,** that is, alters the membrane permeability. Alteration of membrane permeability (polarization) allows a change of electrical charges (negative to positive) that runs along the entire cell membrane. The neuron then returns to its resting electrical state, the resting potential, until stimulated again. *The rate of neural transmission, however, is independent of the level of stimulation.* That is, if the *neural threshold* is not reached, the neuron will not fire. If the threshold is reached or exceeded, the amplitude of the action potential is the same regardless of the level of stimulation.

The relationship between the level of stimulation and the production of a neural impulse is called the **all or none principle.** Once triggered, the action potential continues the length of the axon without diminishing because the action potential depends upon cell membrane permeability, a cell characteristic, and not upon the strength of the triggering stimulus.

After the action potential occurs, however, there is a short period of **refractoriness,** which affects neuron firing. During the first part of the refractory period (the **absolute refractory period**), the neuron will not fire again no matter how great the stimulation. The absolute refractory period lasts for only a short time. It is followed by the **relative refractory period,** during which a stronger than usual stimulus is required to trigger the action potential before the neuron returns to resting state. After the refractory period, the neuron will fire when the neural threshold is reached.

Synaptic transmission. The **synapse** is the name given the junction between neurons where information is exchanged (Figure 2). The action potential causes information to be transmitted from the axon of the first neuron **(presynaptic neuron)** to the dendrites or cell body of the second neuron **(postsynaptic neuron)** by secretion of chemicals called **neurotransmitters. Neurotransmitters** are stored in small containers **(vesicles)** located in knoblike structures **(terminal buttons)** on the axon tips. The axon of the presynaptic neuron does not actually touch the dendrites of the postsynaptic **neuron** and is separated from them by a space called the **synaptic cleft.** Stimulation of the presynaptic neuron to produce an action potential causes the release of neurotransmitters into the synaptic cleft. Most of the released neurotransmitters bind with molecules at special sites, **receptors,** on the dendrites of the postsynaptic neuron. (Molecules of the neurotransmitter that do not bind to receptors in the postsynaptic neuron are taken up again by the presynaptic neuron, a process called **reuptake**).

The combination of the neurotransmitter molecules to receptor cell molecules in the postsynaptic cell membrane produces a change of potential in the postsynaptic cell membrane called the **postsynaptic potential (PSP).** The PSP allows ions to enter or leave the cell membrane of the postsynaptic neuron. The ionic movements increase or decrease the probability of a neural impulse occurring in the postsynaptic neuron. There are two types of PSPs, **excitatory (EPSPs)** and **inhibitory (IPSPs).** EPSPs increase and IPSPs decrease the likelihood that the postsynaptic neuron will fire a neural impulse. The rate of firing of a neuron at a particular time depends upon the relative number of EPSPs and IPSPs.

Neurotransmitters. Many drugs, both therapeutic and recreational, work by affecting the level of **neurotransmitters** (Figure 2) (the chemicals released at the axon terminal buttons of the presynaptic neuron), and some disorders are associated with neurotransmitter deficiencies or excesses. Neurotransmitters are of several types:

- **Acetylcholine** occurs throughout the nervous system and is the only neurotransmitter found in synapses between motor neurons and voluntary muscle cells. (Degeneration of cells producing acetylcholine is associated with Alzheimer's disease.)

- **Biogenic amines** include three neurotransmitters: **norepinephrine, dopamine,** and **serotonin.** Parkinson's disease is believed to be related to a deficiency of dopamine; certain types of depression are associated with low levels of norepinephrine; levels of serotonin increase with the use of the recreational drug LSD (lysergic acid diethylamide).

- **GABA (gamma aminobutyric acid)** appears to produce only inhibitory PSPs. Many tranquilizers work by increasing the inhibitory actions of GABA.

- **Glycine** is an inhibitory neurotransmitter found in the lower brainstem, spinal cord, and retina.

- **Endorphins** modulate the activity of other neurotransmitters and are called **neuromodulators.** They seem to function in the same way as opiates such as morphine; "runner's high" is produced by an increase in endorphins.

- **Substance P** is a neurotransmitter in many neural circuits involving pain.

The Nervous System

The **nervous system** (Figure 4) has two components: the **central nervous system (CNS)** and the **peripheral nervous system (PNS)**.

The Nervous System

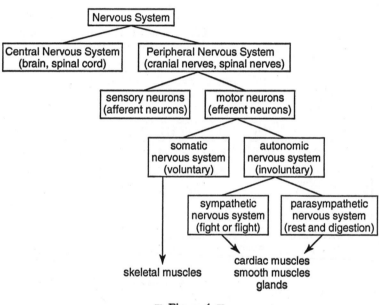

■ Figure 4 ■

The **CNS** consists of the **brain** and the **spinal cord,** which lie within the skull and within the spinal column, respectively; both are bathed in a special fluid called the **cerebrospinal fluid (CSF)** and are protected by enclosing sheaths called **meninges.** The **meninges** consist of three layers: the outer layer (**dura mater**), the middle layer (**arachnoid layer**), and the inner layer (**pia mater**). Below the arachnoid layer and above the pia mater is a space called the **subarachnoid space,** which is filled with cerebrospinal fluid.

The **PNS** consists of the **somatic nervous system** and the **autonomic nervous system,** which is composed of the **sympathetic** and the **parasympathetic nervous systems.**

The Central Nervous System (CNS): The Brain and the Spinal Cord

The **central nervous system (CNS)** (Figure 4) consists of the brain and the spinal cord. Early in its development, the CNS is a hollow tube with three interconnected chambers. During development, the chambers become the **ventricles** (see below), and the tissue around them becomes the three major brain divisions (Table 1).

DIVISIONS OF THE BRAIN			
Divisions	**Ventricle**	**Subdivision**	**Components**
Forebrain (Prosencephalon)	Lateral	Telencephalon	Cerebral cortex Basal ganglia Limbic system
	Third	Diencephalon	Thalamus Hypothalamus

Midbrain (Mesencephalon)	Cerebral aqueduct		Tectum
			  Superior colliculus
			  Inferior colliculus
			
			Tegmentum
			  Midbrain reticular formation

Hindbrain (Rhombencephalon)	Fourth	Metencephalon	Cerebellum Pons Pontine reticular formation
		Myelencephalon	Medulla oblongata

■ Table 1 ■

The brain. The three major parts of the **brain** are

- the **forebrain,** the most recently evolved section
- the **midbrain,** which contains the upper part of the brain stem
- the **hindbrain,** which contains most of the brain stem

The brain has a series of hollow, interconnected chambers called **ventricles.** The **lateral ventricles** are in the forebrain and are connected to the **third ventricle** in the midbrain. The **third ventricle** is connected by way of the **cerebral aqueduct,** a long tube, to the **fourth ventricle** in the hindbrain, which is then connected to the central canal of the spinal cord (Figure 5). The ventricular system provides the pathway for cerebrospinal fluid to move in the nervous system.

The Ventricles and the Three Major Parts of the Brain

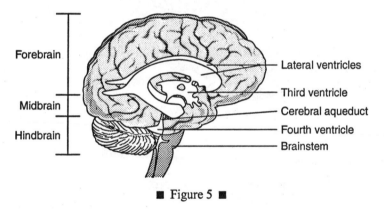

■ Figure 5 ■

The **forebrain (prosencephalon)** consists of two major components: the telencephalon and, below it, the diencephalon.

■ the **telencephalon (cerebrum)** is divided into two left and right symmetrical halves known as **cerebral hemispheres.** Each hemisphere is divided into four areas called **lobes** (Figure 6), which have different functions.

The Lobes of the Brain

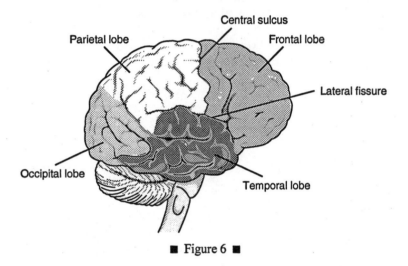

■ Figure 6 ■

—In the **frontal lobe** are the principal areas that control the movement of muscles.

—The **parietal lobe** contains information that regulates somatosensory information (the skin senses of touch, heat, pressure, and pain).

—The **temporal lobe** helps integrate sensory information and some auditory information, including language.

—The **occipital lobe** (back of the head) is the area from which visual signals are sent.

The **central sulcus** divides the frontal lobe from the parietal lobe, and the **lateral fissure** separates the temporal lobe from frontal and parietal lobes (Figure 6). The hemispheres are connected by the **corpus callosum,** the largest **commissure** (cross-hemisphere connection) of the brain.

The cerebral hemispheres are covered with a layer of cells called the **cerebral cortex** and contain the **basal ganglia** and the **limbic system.**

— The **cerebral cortex** consists of cell bodies, dendrites, the interconnecting axons of neurons, and glial cells (supporting cells). The neurons give the cortex a gray color (hence the name **gray matter.** Cells connecting to the cortex contain a large concentration of myelin, which is white, and are called **white matter.**) In humans, the cortex has many convolutions that consist of **sulci** (small grooves), **fissures** (large grooves), and **gyri** (bulges between adjacent sulci or fissures). Most of the cortex is hidden in these grooves.

— Below the cortex are the **basal ganglia,** a collection of subcortical nuclei that are involved in movement. (Degeneration of these structures is associated with Parkinson's disease.)

— The **limbic system** is a collection of numerous brain areas involved in emotion expression. Among the system's structures are the portion of the cortex known as the **rhinencephalon,** which contains the **anterior thalamus, amygdala, septal area, cingulate gyrus,** and **hippocampus** (a structure involved in the processing of memories, particularly short-term memory). The limbic system also includes neural connections to the **hypothalamus.**

■ The **diencephalon,** the lower portion of the forebrain, contains the thalamus, and hypothalamus (Figure 7).

— The **thalamus** is a structure through which all sensory information except olfaction (smell) must pass.

—The **hypothalamus** is below the thalamus and contains structures that regulate the biological drives (for example, hunger or thirst).

Sagittal Section of the Brain

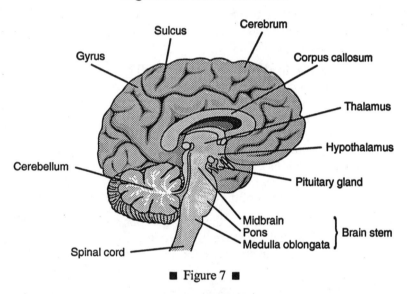

■ Figure 7 ■

The **midbrain (mesencephalon,** Figure 7) (located between the forebrain and hindbrain) helps regulate sensory processes (such as locating the position of objects in space) and is the location of the dopamine systems involved with performance of voluntary movements. (Damage to these dopaminergic systems may result in Parkinson's disorder.) The midbrain also contains the **tectum** (which contains the **superior** and **inferior colliculi,** primitive centers for vision and hearing) and the **tegmentum** (which contains the **midbrain reticular formation,** part of the **reticular formation,** a structure that runs through both the midbrain and hindbrain and is involved in certain muscle reflexes, pain perception, and breathing).

The **hindbrain (rhombencephalon)** includes the metencephalon and the myelencephalon.

- The **metencephalon** contains the cerebellum and the pons (Figure 7).

  —The **cerebellum** is a large structure in the lower back of the brain that coordinates movement and equilibrium.

  —The **pons** (which means "bridge") has fibers that connect the brain stem to the cerebellum and also has groups of cells that are important in sleep and arousal, the **pontine reticular formation.**

- The **myelencephalon** is below the pons and contains the **medulla oblongata,** a structure involved with functions such as breathing, swallowing, regulation of heart rate, and other important functions essential to life.

Brain stem is a term used to identify certain brain structures; it consists of the midbrain and parts of the hindbrain (pons and medulla) and connects the spinal cord to the forebrain (Figure 7).

The spinal cord. The **spinal cord** connects the brain to the rest of the body through the peripheral nervous system. The spinal cord is connected to the brain through an opening in the base of the skull and extends to a point just below the waist. It is covered by meninges and is contained within the bones (**vertebrae**) of the spinal column.

The Peripheral Nervous System (PNS)

The **peripheral nervous system (PNS)** (Figure 4) has two components: the somatic nervous system and the autonomic nervous system. The PNS consists of all of the nerves that lie outside the brain and spinal cord. **Nerves** are bundles of neuron fibers (axons) that are grouped together to carry information to and from the same structure.

- **The somatic nervous system.** The **somatic nervous system** is made up of nerves that connect to voluntary skeletal muscles and to sensory receptors. It is composed of **afferent** nerves that carry information to the central nervous system (spinal cord) and **efferent** fibers that carry neural impulses away from the central nervous system.

- The **autonomic nervous system** also consists of two components: the sympathetic division and the parasympathetic division. This system mediates much of the physiological arousal (such as rapid heart beat, tremor, or sweat) experienced by a fearful person in an emergency situation.

  — The **sympathetic nervous system** mobilizes the body to respond to emergencies.

  — The **parasympathetic nervous system** generally helps to conserve the body's energy. It controls normal operations of the body such as digestion, blood pressure, and heart rate. It helps the body return to normal activity after an emergency.

The Endocrine System

Communication from the brain is sent to the rest of the body by the endocrine system as well as by the nervous system. The **endocrine system** is a series of glands throughout the body that secrete chemicals (**hormones**) into the bloodstream; hormones, in turn, affect body functions. (The endocrine system and its role in stress and health is discussed also beginning on page 92.) The endocrine glands, their locations, and their major functions are given in Table 2.

LOCATIONS AND MAJOR FUNCTIONS OF THE ENDOCRINE GLANDS		
Endocrine Gland	**Location**	**Function**
Pituitary gland Anterior	Brain	Secretes growth hormones and regulates secretions of thyroid gland, pancreas, adrenal cortex, and gonads
Posterior	Brain	Regulates water and salt metabolism
Thyroid gland	Throat	Regulates metabolic rates
Pancreas	Abdomen	Secretes insulin and glucagon to regulate sugar metabolism
Adrenal glands Adrenal cortex	Top of kidneys	Affects salt and carbohydrate metabolism and inflammatory reactions
Adrenal medulla	Top of kidneys	Affects sleep and emotional arousal
Gonads Ovaries (female)	Lower abdomen	Secretes sex hormones
Testes (male)	Scrotum	Secretes sex hormones

■ Table 2 ■

Heredity

Biology affects behavior also through mechanisms of **heredity** regulated by **genetic principles.** The **nature versus nurture** controversy—that is, how much of our behavior is due to inherited factors and how much to environmental factors—is a question that has plagued scientists for years and is still unresolved.

Genetic principles. **Genetics** is the study of **heredity,** the manner in which traits and characteristics (for example, eye color) are passed from parent to offspring. Each human cell, except sex cells, contains 23 pairs of **chromosomes,** a total of 46. (Sex cells—the sperm and the egg—each contain 23 chromosomes but form a total of 46 when they unite.) Chromosomes are strands of DNA (deoxyribonucleic acid) in the nuclei of cells that carry genetic information, **genes.**

Genetic studies in psychology. Researchers in the field called **behavioral genetics** study, through both family and twin studies, the way in which genetic factors affect behavioral traits. In **family studies,** the focus is on the investigation of blood relatives to see how similar they are with respect to some trait (for example, the occurrence of a mental disorder such as schizophrenia). **Twin studies** compare identical twins and fraternal twins for various similarities in appearance and behavior to see which traits/behaviors are affected by genetic makeup. In some cases when twins have been adopted into separate families, it is possible to expand the information and determine which traits are affected by environment rather than heredity.

Studies of **genetic defects** (for example, certain types of developmental disabilities) also provide pertinent information on the effects of heredity/environment upon behavior.

- **Down syndrome** is a human genetic defect in which there is an extra 21st chromosome. People with Down syndrome have distinctive physical features and often some type of developmental disability.

- **Phenylketonuria (PKU)** is an inherited metabolic disorder. The presence of a particular gene keeps the individual from being able to process the amino acid phenylalanine. An excess of this chemical interferes with the formation of myelin in the brain and can produce a type of developmental disability. The genetic problem can be detected by a PKU test given at birth and can be regulated by dietary methods.

Learning about the Brain

Both surgical procedures and those involving measurement, have been used to understand the way the brain functions.

Bisecting the brain. The brain may be **bisected**—that is, split into two hemispheres by severing the corpus callosum—for medical reasons (such as to treat epilepsy, or to remove tumors). After such a procedure, it is possible to compare the functioning of the left and right hemispheres (that is, to study **cerebral laterality**). For example, studies have been conducted showing the relationship of the hemisphere used and handedness (left or right) and hemisphere used and gender (whether males or females use one hemisphere or the other more). Cerebral laterality studies are conducted also in the absence of brain bisection by using special types of laboratory equipment that can block sensory input to one hemisphere.

Lesioning. Lesioning, the destruction of a portion of the brain (through strokes, accidents, or surgical procedures), helps identify the function associated with that portion of the brain.

Electrical stimulation of the brain. Electrodes can be implanted to very precise positions in the brain. Administration of small amounts of electric current into a brain structure helps identify its function. (These functions and their role in motivation are discussed beginning on page 77.)

Brain imaging procedures. Several **brain imaging** procedures have been used medically in recent years to identify problem areas in the brain.

- The **CT (computerized tomography)** is a computer-enhanced x-ray of the brain.

- **PET scans (positron emission tomography)** are used to map brain activity.

- **MRI (magnetic resonance imaging)** makes use of radio waves, magnetic fields, and enhancement by computers to show three-dimensional pictures.

Monitoring brain activity. Brain activity can be monitored by inserting electrodes into single neurons and recording single cell activity in laboratory studies. Activity of the entire brain can be measured through **electroencephalography,** a technique that records from electrodes placed on the scalp and produces a pattern of brain waves called an **electroencephalogram.** The procedure is used in both research and medicine. Upon examination of the frequency and amplitude of the brain waves, it is possible for an expert to differentiate between sleep and waking activity as well as to detect certain pathological conditions such as an epileptic seizure or a brain tumor.

The nervous system receives input through an array of sense organs (for example, the eye, ear, or nose) and transforms the information into neural processes through a procedure called **sensation.** (Using the computer analogy, sensation can be compared to computer input.) Each sensory system (vision, hearing, taste, olfaction, and the cutaneous (skin) senses of pressure, temperature, and pain) is described separately below, but all follow similar principles for the conversion of a physical stimulus into a psychological experience.

Sensory Thresholds

Receptors for each sensory system are limited by the amount of stimulation necessary to elicit a sensation and by the amount of stimulus change that can be detected. In the field of psychology called **psychophysics,** relationships between physical stimuli and psychological experience are studied. One technique to study such relationships is called the **method of constant stimuli,** in which stimuli of varying intensities are presented in random order to a subject. The results are used to determine the **absolute threshold**—the minimum intensity detected by a subject 50% of the time. (Your dog, for instance, has a much lower absolute threshold for sound than you do and hears a car in the driveway before you hear the knock on the door.)

The **difference threshold**—the minimum (physical) distinction between stimulus attributes that can be detected 50% of the time—is also of concern. The difference threshold is also called a **just noticeable difference (JND).** Ernst Weber, a well-known early investigator, observed that regardless of their magnitude, two stimuli must differ by a constant proportion for their difference to be detectable. His observations are formulated as **Weber's law,** which states that the "just noticeable difference" is a constant fraction of the stimulus intensity already present. (If a room is quiet, you can hear a faint knock at the door. But if your CD player is blaring, it takes a loud bang on the door for you to hear it.) If you are exposed to a stimulus that doesn't change over a period of time, **sensory adaptation** occurs, and you become less sensitive to the stimulus. If you have to study in a room with a constant noise outside, for example, you will usually eventually adapt to the noise, and it will become less offensive.

Signal detection. Factors other than the magnitude of the stimulus also affect sensory discriminations. When a discrimination—that is, the detection of a stimulus (a signal)—must be made against a background of noise, the procedure is called **signal detection.** Signal detection theory takes into account the fact that people are making decisions as they make sensory discriminations. When they attempt to separate a signal change from its background, they may guess, have biases in their judgments, or become less vigilant during the judging process. Knowledge of signal detection theory is useful in many situations— for instance, if one were teaching people to detect accurately small blips on radar screens in an air control tower. Another aspect of sensory perception, **subliminal perception** (perception without awareness), has been of interest in recent years. However, the data concerning the existence of the phenomenon are still controversial.

Vision

Light. The stimulus for **vision** is **light,** which travels in waves. The **amplitude** (wave height) is associated with the sensory experience of **brightness;** the **wavelength** determines the **hue** (color) of the light; and the **wave purity** (whether there is more than one type of wave) produces the psychological experience of **saturation.**

The vision system. Light travels to the eye and passes through the **cornea,** the **pupil** (regulated in size by the **iris**), and the **lens** and then moves to the **retina,** where it strikes the photoreceptors for vision, the cones and the rods. The **cones**, in the center (**fovea**) of the retina, are responsible for color vision, and operate best in intense illumination. The **rods** are important for night vision and peripheral vision and have a greater density at the edge of the retina. Visual information proceeds from the eye through **optic nerves** attached to the retina at the back of each eye; the optic nerves meet and then divide at the **optic chiasm** in the center of the brain (Figure 8). The lateral portion of each optic nerve travels from the optic chiasm to the lateral **visual cortex** on the same side of the brain (that is, the outside of the right nerve to right visual cortex and the outside of the left nerve to the left visual cortex). However, the medial portion of each nerve crosses over at the optic chiasm and goes to the medial visual cortex on the other side of the brain (medial right nerve to left medial visual cortex and medial left nerve to right medial visual cortex).

The Visual Pathway

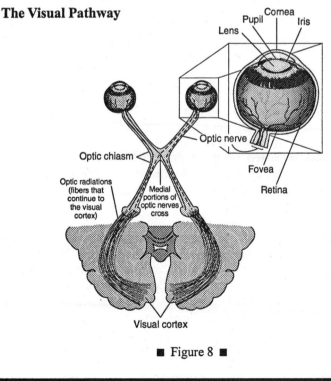

■ Figure 8 ■

Color vision. The three **primary colors** are **red, green,** and **blue.** Two theories suggest the way the eye functions in color vision.

- The **Young-Helmholtz trichromatic theory of color vision,** proposed by Thomas Young and Hermann von Helmholtz, states that the eye has three types of cones with different sensitivities to lights of different wavelengths that produce the primary hues of red, green, and blue.

- Ewald Hering, feeling that the Young-Helmholtz theory did not cover all visual phenomena, offered the **opponent process theory** to explain visual images that are the complementary color of the image of the stimulus. For example, if you stare at a red dot and then look at a white paper, you will see the afterimage of a blue-green dot. (Blue-green is the complementary color of red.) These theories help to explain some of types of color blindness (some people, dichromats, have a hard time telling green from red or yellow from blue).

Hearing

Sound. **Sound,** the stimulus for **hearing,** is made up of a series of pressures, usually of air, that can be represented as waves. **Sound waves** have three characteristics—amplitude, frequency, and purity— each of which is related to a psychological experience. Greater wave **amplitudes** are related to greater **loudness; wave frequency** is related to **pitch;** and **wave purity** is related to **timbre.**

The hearing system. The **outer ear,** the **pinna,** collects sound waves and funnels them through the **auditory canal** to the **eardrum** (which separates the outer and middle ears) and causes it to vibrate. (See Figure 9.) The **middle ear** contains the **malleus (hammer), incus (anvil),** and **stapes (stirrup),** which move and transmit the sound to the **oval window,** which separates the middle ear from the inner ear. Beyond the oval window is the **inner ear,** whose main structure is the **cochlea,** a

snail-like structure that has a membrane, the **basilar membrane,** stretched along its length. When the stapes vibrates against the oval window, the fluid in the cochlea moves and causes the basilar membrane to vibrate. The receptors for hearing, the **hair cells,** lie in the basilar membrane and convert the vibrations into **neural impulses.** The neural impulses, in turn, move along the **auditory nerve** to the lower **brain stem** and then ascend to the auditory part of the **thalamus** and on to the **auditory cortex** in the temporal lobe. Input from each ear is received on both sides of the brain.

The Ear

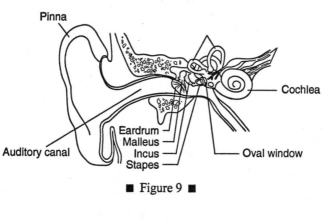

■ Figure 9 ■

The Chemical Senses: Taste and Smell

Taste. The stimuli for **taste** are chemical substances dissolved in water or other fluids. Taste can be described as four basic sensations, **sweet, sour, salty,** and **bitter,** which can be combined in various ways to make all other taste sensations. Taste receptors (called **taste buds**) for these sensations are located primarily on various areas of the tongue: front, sweet; sides, sour; sides and front, salty; and back, bitter (Figure 10). There are about 10,000 taste buds, which are situated primarily in or around the bumps (**papillae**) on the tongue. Each **papilla** contains several taste buds, from which information is sent by **afferent nerves** to the **thalamus** and, ultimately, to areas in the cortex.

Taste Receptors

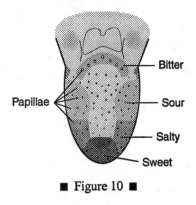

■ Figure 10 ■

Smell (olfaction). The stimuli for **smell** are volatile chemical substances suspended in the air. These molecules stimulate the **olfactory receptors,** which are in the upper portions of the nasal passages. Neurons from these receptors bundle together to form the **olfactory nerve,** which travels to the **olfactory bulb** at the base of the brain. The theory of smell is not well understood (for example, how an odor of apple pie can evoked pleasant childhood memories).

The Cutaneous (Skin) Senses

The **skin** contains receptors that respond to touch, pressure, and temperature. The relationships between receptors and the cutaneous sensations are not completely understood. **Meissner's corpuscles** are sensitive to touch and **Pacinian corpuscles** to deep pressure. **Ruffini endings** transmit information about warmth and **Krause's bulbs** about cold. Information is transmitted from the receptors to **nerve fibers** that are routed through the **spinal cord** to the **brainstem.** From there they are transmitted to an area of cortex in the **parietal lobe.** Skin senses also undergo various kinds of sensory adaptation. For example, a hot tub can be initially so hot that it is intolerable, but after awhile one can sit in it without discomfort.

Pain. Pain receptors are mostly free nerve endings in the skin. Information is transmitted by two types of pathways to the **brain** by way of the **thalamus.**

- The **fast pathway (myelinated)** detects localized pain and sends that information rapidly to the cortex.

- The **slow pathway (unmyelinated)** carries less-localized, longer-acting pain information (such as that concerning chronic aches).

Many of the neural circuits that deliver pain signals to the brain and the spinal cord use **substance P** as a neurotransmitter (p. 22). In addition, chemicals in the body called **endorphins** (chemicals with actions similar to those of morphine) increase in concentration when the body is responding to pain by serving as **neuromodulators** (chemicals that increase or decrease—modulate—the activity of specific neurotransmitters).

The **gate control theory of pain,** proposed by Ronald Melzack, proposes that a "neurological gate" in the spinal cord controls the transmission of pain impulses to the brain. Determination of whether the gate is open or closed depends upon a complex competition between different types of nerve fibers.

Acupuncture is a procedure developed by the Chinese for controlling pain by the insertion of long needles in various parts of the body. Although it is not known precisely how acupuncture alleviates pain, one theory suggests that the needles activate large nerve fibers and close the pain gate, while another suggests that the needles cause the release of endorphins, which serve as analgesics.

The Vestibular Senses

Awareness of body balance and movement are monitored by the **vestibular system.** The **vestibular senses** (the sensations of body rotation and of gravitation and movement) arise in the inner ear; the sense organs are the hair cells that send out signals over the auditory nerve.

The sensation of **body rotation** arises in the three **semicircular canals** in the inner ear. Movement of fluid in the canals stimulates hair cells, which send messages to the brain about speed and direction of body rotation. **Gravitation** and **movement** sensations are produced by movement of two **vestibular sacs** in each ear that lie between the semicircular canal and the cochlea. Both sacs are filled with millions of tiny crystals that bend hair cells when moved. In turn, impulses giving a sense of position are sent to the brain. (Motion sickness originates from excessive stimulation of the vestibular organs.

The Kinesthetic System

Movement of the body's muscles, tendons, and joints is also monitored by **mechanoreceptors** in these structures. The process is called **kinesthesis.**

Perception is the way that sensory information is chosen and transformed so that it has meaning. Once sensory input starts, an individual uses perceptual processes to select among sensory input stimuli and to organize them so that relevant action can occur. (In the computer analogy, the process of perception would represent use of both hardware and software in the central nervous system; many of the perceptual processes are innate—hardware—but some may be modified—software.)

Stimulus Input: Attention and Set

Attention. Too many events occur simultaneously in the environment to pay attention to all of them at once, so **selective attention** is used to focus on those stimuli relevant to current activity. (For example, you might not generally pay much attention to wind direction, but you do if you're flying a kite or hitting a golf ball.)

Set. In terms of perception, a **set,** a predisposition to respond in a particular fashion, may be one of several types.

- **Motor set.** When attending to a stimulus, an individual organizes muscular responses, a **motor set,** to be ready for the particular attention situation. For example, a golfer getting ready to hit a golf ball adopts a particular posture and a practiced way of holding the golf club; similarly, members of basketball teams adopt particular stances, motor sets, as they stand lined up and ready to jump while waiting for the free throw.

- **Perceptual set.** A **perceptual set** is the readiness to interpret a stimulus in a certain way. For example, if you have just run a red traffic light, you might be more inclined to view a flashing light as a police car than as just a bright turn signal. (Note that perceptual sets occur in all of the sensory modalities, not just vision.)

- **Mental set.** A **mental set** is a predisposition to think about a situation or a problem in a specific way. For example, a student's poor performance on a math assignment might be because of lack of preparation or because of the mental set "I just can't do well on math problems."

Stimulus characteristics that affect set. A variety of stimulus characteristics affect perception and the set that is formed.

- **Stimulus intensity.** If other stimulus factors are comparable, a more **intense stimulus** attracts more attention than does a more subtle one. For example, a loud siren gets more attention than a faint one.

- **Stimulus changes. Stimulus changes** elicit more attention than does sameness or monotony. A flashing light, for example, stands out in a horizon of steady city lights.

- **Stimulus magnitude. Stimulus magnitude** is also a factor in attracting attention. For example, a large advertising billboard attracts more attention than a small one.

- **Stimulus repetition.** A **repeated stimulus** affects attention; the public quickly recognizes a product seen in repeated advertisements.

Organization of Perceptions

The manner in which stimuli are arranged, that is, **grouped,** (in addition to their individual characteristics) also affects their perception.

Stimulus characteristics that affect organization. Important stimulus characteristics that affect the organization of stimuli and their perception include the following:

- **Closure. Closure** is the completion of an incomplete stimulus. If someone yells at you, "Close the _____," the word *door* isn't said, but you fill in the blank because of past experience and close the door.

- **Nearness.** Stimuli that are **near** one another tend to be grouped together; stars near one another are sometimes seen as a pattern or constellation, which is not the case for stars that are far apart.

- **Similarity.** Stimuli that are **similar** to one another are frequently grouped together; people wearing the same band uniforms are seen as similar compared to a group of marching people wearing everyday clothes.

- **Continuity.** The tendency is to view a figure, pattern, or illustration that contains gaps as smooth and **continuous** rather than as discontinuous. The broken line down the middle of the highway is perceived as a continuous dotted line rather than a long row of blocks.

- **Contiguity. Contiguity,** or nearness in time and space, also influences perception. If certain theme songs and visual stimuli are placed near the beginning or end of television programs, these stimuli are associated with the starting or stopping of the program.

Perceptual Constancy

There is a tendency to maintain **constancy** (of **size, color,** and **shape**) in the perception of stimuli even though the stimuli have changed. For example, you recognize that small brownish dog in the distance as your neighbor's large golden retriever, so you aren't surprised by the great increase in size (**size constancy**) or the appearance of the yellow color (**color constancy**) when he comes bounding up. And in spite of the changes in the appearance of the dog moving toward you from a distance, you still perceive the shape as that of a dog (**shape constancy**) no matter the angle from which it is viewed.

Depth and Distance Perception

Perceptual processes function in the three-dimensional organization of stimuli as well as in distance judgments. The processes include use of both monocular and binocular cues.

Monocular cues. Monocular cues, those used when looking at objects with one eye closed, help an individual to form a three-dimensional concept of the stimulus object. Such cues include

- **size** of the stimulus

- **interposition,** when one stimulus blocks the image of another

- **shadows,** which indicate distance

- **linear perspective,** the convergence of parallel tracks or lines as they recede into the distance

- **texture changes** (distinct bricks are seen in a near wall but become a pattern with increased distance)

- **relative motion (motion parallax),** used in judging distance (when you are traveling in a car, near objects seen out the window seem to move rapidly, but far ones don't seem to move)

Binocular cues. Binocular cues, those used when looking at objects with both eyes, also function in depth perception. Examples are

- **retinal disparity,** the differences in images on the retinas of the two eyes

- **eye convergence,** a necessary visual response in order to focus on a distant object

Illusions. Presentation of multiple stimuli elicits a tendency to group some of them together and others apart, a phenomenon which can create optical **illusions.** An example is the **Müller-Lyer illusion** shown in Figure 11. The lengths of the two lines appear to be different but are the same.

The Müller-Lyer Illusion

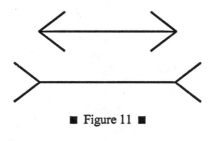

■ Figure 11 ■

Other Factors Influencing Perception

Personal characteristics. Personal characteristics, such as past experience (learning) and motivation, may also affect the way stimuli are perceived.

- **Learning** (a musician quickly learns the pattern of tones that make a melody and detects a discordant note)

- **Motivation** (while an individual may not initially have a taste for espresso coffee, if the person's group of acquaintances perceives it as an "in" beverage, he or she may then start drinking espresso)

Gestalt Theory

A group of early experimental psychologists known as **Gestalt** psychologists (p. 3) believed that perceptions are more than the stimuli that create them. By *more* is meant that a meaningful, whole pattern is created by the stimuli (that is, the total is more than the sum of its parts). These psychologists developed the idea, the principle of **Prägnanz,** that stimuli can be grouped and seen as a whole. These psychologists believed that the innate, organizing tendencies of the brain would explain organization functions in perception, including many optical illusions, for example, the phi phenomenon and certain figure-ground relationships.

- The **phi phenomenon** occurs when you see two adjacent lights alternately blinking off and on and perceive them as one light moving back and forth. This phi phenomenon illusion is frequently used in signs to suggest movement.

- **Figure (object)–ground (background)** relationships are important in Gestalt theory, which suggests that perceptions are organized to produce a figure-ground effect. One tends to see objects against backgrounds rather than to view each separately. However, when instructed, one may reverse the relationship and see the object as background and vice versa. In the famous figure-ground illustration shown in Figure 12, do you see a goblet or the profile of two faces?

A Figure-Ground Illustration

■ Figure 12 ■

Extrasensory Perception

A phenomenon related to the study of perception and well known in the popular domain is called **extrasensory perception (ESP).** The belief is that one can have a perceptual experience without any sensory input. Types of reported ESPs include

- **mental telepathy,** the ability to read another person's thoughts

- **forecasting,** the ability to predict future incidents accurately (for example, who will win a race or engage in a particular activity)

- **clairvoyance,** the awareness of some event that one cannot see (for example, knowing where a body is hidden)

- **psychokinesis,** the ability to cause things to move by virtue of thought processes

Psychologists known as **parapsychologists** study these phenomena, but the majority of psychologists feel that evidence for the existence of ESP phenomena has not been adequately documented.

Consciousness is the *awareness* of stimuli (both internal and external) and events. Awareness, however—both of internal psychological functioning and of external environmental factors—can change, and responses can vary widely as a result of an individual's level of consciousness. Imagine, for example, the response of a wide-awake person to a knock on the door compared to that of a drunk person or one wakcd from a deep sleep. All living creatures undergo changes in levels of awareness throughout a 24-hour period. Examples are the sleep-wake cycles and the changes in biological cycles called circadian rhythms. Consequently, to understand the science of behavior and mental processes, psychologists must also understand the effects of levels of awareness (consciousness)on psychological functioning.

Historical Background

Early investigations of consciousness. Psychologists have been concerned with the study of consciousness since Wilhelm Wundt conducted studies on the subject at the University of Leipzig in 1879. William James in 1890 described the mind as a **stream of consciousness,** a continuous flow of changing images, sensations, feelings, and thoughts. (To illustrate for yourself the concept of stream of consciousness, simply keep track of all your thoughts and feelings for 5 minutes, particularly while in class.) Edward Titchener (1867–1927) used a technique called **introspection,** whereby individuals could be trained to analyze conscious experiences. Sigmund Freud (1856–1939) was particularly interested in the *lack* of consciousness, the unconscious. Freud believed that the **unconscious** is a reservoir of unacceptable thoughts, wishes, and feelings that are beyond conscious awareness and that can be reached by psychoanalytic techniques. (See p. 146.)

Sleep

All species engage in periods (cycles) of sleeping and wakefulness. In part, these cycles are regulated by the nervous system, specifically by a structure in the hypothalamus called the **suprachiasmatic nucleus**. The **reticular activating system,** an aggregate of cells in the central part of the brain stem, also affects arousal. Other areas in the medulla and thalamus have also been implicated in the control of sleep and waking. When one is sleeping, responses to environmental stimulation are altered and produce different levels of awareness.

Sleep records. Several types of machines can record bodily changes, including activity of the brain, muscles, and eyes, that occur during sleep.

- An **EEG (electroencephalogram)** is a record (made by attaching electrodes to the scalp and face) of patterns of brain activity during periods of sleep and\or waking. EEG records are used to study the sleep process. Records of activity patterns during sleep are different from those obtained during periods of wakefulness. The sleep wave patterns have been characterized by their frequencies, cycles per second:

    —**beta waves,** 14 to 30 cycles per second

    —**alpha waves,** 8 to 13 cycles per second

    —**theta waves,** 4 to 7 cycles per second

    —**delta waves,** under 4 cycles per second

Brain waves also differ in amplitude (wave height). As one falls asleep, brain waves become slower in frequency and higher in amplitude.

- An **EMG (electromyogram)** is a record of muscular tension or relaxation. The device uses electrodes attached beneath the chin.

- An **EOG (electro-oculogram)** is a record of eye movement and is made by means of electrodes attached near the outer corners of the eyes.

All three devices may be used in sleep research laboratories.

Stages of sleep. There are four stages of sleep plus a condition called REM (rapid eye movement) sleep.

- **Stage one** sleep is a relaxed wakefulness, with EEG activity of 8 to 13 cycles per second called **alpha waves.** Eye movement occurs as well as muscular tension.

- **Stage two** sleep is marked by bursts of activity called **sleep spindles,** which occur at approximately 15-second intervals. Muscle tension is reduced; no eye movement occurs. This stage lasts approximately 20 minutes.

- **Stage three** sleep lasts for about 30 minutes; some **delta waves** occur. Temperature decreases and pulse and breathing rate slow.

- **Stage four** sleep is the deepest and consists almost exclusively of **delta waves.** Eyes do not move.

During sleep, a person moves through sleep stages one to four; the sleep cycle then reverses back through stages three and two to stage one (which, in the reverse order, is called **emergent stage one**). This cycle generally repeats several times during a night's sleep. As a sleeper passes on through stage two and back into stage one, the eyes begin to dart back and forth; **REM (rapid eye movement)** sleep and **dreams** occur. (REM sleep is also called **paradoxical** sleep because the brain activity, blood pressure, heart rate, etc., closely resemble those of waking consciousness.) Because neither dreams nor rapid eye movements occur in any of the other stages of sleep, those stages are called **NREM (non-rapid eye movement)** sleep.

Sleep deprivation. When people go without sleep (**sleep deprivation**), especially if they have missed REM sleep, drastic changes in their behavior patterns occur. Sleep-deprived people become tired, irritable, and lethargic.

Dreams. Analysis of **dreams,** which occur during REM sleep, is an important part of the psychoanalytic treatment for emotional problems. During the treatment process, patients report what they consciously remember about their dreams, the **manifest content.** In order to better understand their emotional problems, the analyst then has them use a process called free association to help determine the **latent content** (unconscious portion) of the dream.

Daydreams. **Daydreams,** as well as sleep, indicate an altered level of consciousness. They represent a shift in attention from ongoing events. People daydream most frequently at night just before they go to bed, but they may daydream any time, especially when engaged in a monotonous task. Daydreams have value because they provide relief from boredom through continuous and frequently changing stimulation; in addition, they permit the planning and imaginary trying out of solutions to problems.

Sleep disorders. The term **sleep disorders** refers to a variety of problems people have with the process of sleeping.

- One of the most serious conditions is **sleep apnea,** a sometimes fatal disorder in which people momentarily stop breathing. At the least, this disruption of the breathing process causes the person to be sleepy the next day.

- **Narcolepsy,** another serious sleep disorder, is a condition in which people suddenly fall asleep, even in the middle of another activity.

- **Insomnia,** a common problem, is difficulty in falling asleep.

- **Somnambulism** is sleepwalking.
- **Nightmares** are bad dreams from which the sleeper may wake up aroused and frightened.

Circadian Rhythms

Circadian rhythms are the regular changes in biological processes that follow rhythmical patterns over a 24-hour period. These rhythms involve, in addition to sleep-wake cycles, changes in other body functions, such as the rise and fall of body temperature and blood pressure. Although connected to alternation of night and day, the rhythms are retained (although in 25- rather than 24-hour periods) even when people are forced to adapt to unusual cycles of light and dark, such as those in Antarctica. Animal species other than humans also maintain circadian rhythms, but there are species differences. Horses, cattle, and cats, for example, spend much more time sleeping than do humans. But of particular interest to psychologists are the effects of circadian rhythms on human response to environmental stimulation (that is, on levels of consciousness).

Procedures for Changing Consciousness

Internal processes. Modifications of internal processes, in addition to sleep and dreaming, may be used to change an individual's level of consciousness.

- **Hypnosis** is a procedure whereby the hypnotist creates in a subject a relaxed, highly suggestible state.
- In **meditation,** a person narrows her or his span of attention to produce feelings of relaxation.
- In **biofeedback,** a procedure related to meditation, an individual uses techniques to measure bodily processes—for example,

heart rate, skin temperature, or brain waves—and learns to modify them, usually in a way that promotes relaxation.

External processes. External factors, particularly chemicals such as drugs, may also affect levels of consciousness. Environmental factors such as poor ventilation may influence chemical effects. Chemical substances (**drugs**) are often used in both medical procedures and daily life primarily to change levels of consciousness.

- In medical procedures, chemicals called **general anesthetics (halothane, nitrous oxide,** and others) are used to produce the state of total unconsciousness needed for major surgery.

- **Analgesic drugs,** such as **morphine** and other **opiates** and **aspirin,** are used to reduce pain; morphine and the opiates can also cause changes in mood and can become **addictive.** An addicted person becomes dependent on a drug or drugs and suffers discomfort when it or they are not available. In addition, **tolerance** to the drug(s) occurs, and larger and larger doses are required to produce the same state of relaxation or euphoria.

- **Tranquilizers (antianxiety drugs)** are among the most consistently prescribed mood-altering (in this case, anxiety-reducing) drugs. These drugs include such substances as the **benzodiazepines,** which include the well-known drug **Valium (diazepam).**

- **Depressants** have a relaxing and calming effect. They include such substances as the **barbiturates** and **ethyl alcohol,** widely used as a recreational beverage in beer, wine, and liquor. Both barbiturates and alcohol can be addictive.

- **Stimulants** increase activity in the central nervous system. Examples of stimulants are **cocaine, amphetamine, nicotine,** and **caffeine.**

    —**Cocaine** and **amphetamine** both block the reuptake of neurotransmitters and produce feelings of euphoria; both have been used for medical purposes. Cocaine injections can be used to produce local anesthesia, but **crack cocaine** (which users generally smoke) and **cocaine** per se (which is usually injected) are used as recreational/street drugs and can be addictive.

—**Amphetamines** are stimulants that produce feelings of alertness; they are prescribed as a diet aid and to treat narcolepsy and Parkinson's disease, but they also are used as street drugs, where they are called *speed, uppers,* or *bennies.* They affect the reuptake of the neurotransmitter dopamine and, when taken incorrectly, can create symptoms similar to those sometimes seen in a mental disorder known as schizophrenia.

—**Nicotine** is found in cigarettes. The difficulty of breaking the smoking habit is well known.

—**Caffeine** is, of course, found in coffee, tea, and a number of soft drinks. Many people depend on their morning caffeine jolt.

■ **Hallucinogens** produce mood and behavioral changes that mimic psychotic behaviors. The hallucinogen **LSD (lysergic acid diethylamide)** is a compound that interferes with the reuptake of the neurotransmitter serotonin. Other examples of hallucinogens are **PCP (phencyclidine,** also known as *angel dust)* and **marijuana (tetrahydrocannabinol).**

■ **Designer drugs** are illicitly manufactured variations of known recreational drugs such as opiates, stimulants, or hallucinogens. An example is **MDMA** (known as *ecstasy)*, a substance related to the hallucinogens and amphetamines. Designer drugs frequently contain contaminants or other impurities.

Prenatal/Perinatal Drug Effects

The use of drugs, particularly drugs such as alcohol, cocaine, or marijuana, by either parent at the time of conception or by the mother during the gestation period and\or the lactation period can have serious, long-term effects. Much has been reported about **fetal alcohol babies** and **crack-** or **cocaine-exposed babies** and the problems they present. One of those problems concerns their abilities to respond appropriately to various environmental stimuli. In fact, cocaine-exposed infants are often so overstimulated by ordinary environmental stimuli that they cannot tolerate even being held or comforted. Some fetal alcohol babies, on the other hand, appear less responsive than unexposed infants and may suffer various mental impairments and atypical facial features.

Learning is a relatively permanent behavioral change that occurs as the result of experience. The several types of learning differ from one another in the procedures and elements needed to produce learning. To understand learning, it is important to establish what factors are required for it to occur, not to occur, or to disappear (be **extinguished**).

Responsiveness

Changes in **responsiveness** to stimulus variations can occur in even the simplest organisms on a temporary basis, but these changes are *not* learning. Changes in responsiveness include sensitization and habituation.

- Sometimes the magnitude of responses to stimuli increases after repeated stimulus exposures, a process called **sensitization.** For example, after a series of car engine problems, a driver may become very alert when there is a change in engine sounds, sounds that might formerly have been ignored.

- Conversely, one may become used to a repeated stimulus, for example a radio in the room next door, and become **habituated** (display decreased responsiveness) to the noise.

Although these changes are temporary and thus not classified by most theorists as true learning, they are recognized changes in behavior. Changes in behavior can occur also when one is very tired or is experiencing a marked change (increase or decrease) in motivation, such as that provided by extreme hunger. These changes in behavioral responsiveness also are not learning; that is, they are not relatively permanent changes in behavior as a result of experience. The basic types of learning include classical conditioning, operant conditioning, contingency learning, and cognitive learning.

Classical Conditioning

Classical (Pavlovian) conditioning, first studied by Ivan Pavlov, is a four-step learning procedure involving reflexes. Pavlov became curious about the fact that some of his laboratory dogs began salivating before food actually was in their mouths. He then found that if he used the appropriate sequence of events, a dog would salivate at the sound of a buzzer or the appearance of a light. Further experimentation established the conditions essential in producing such a phenomenon.

Classical conditioning requires the existence of an **unconditioned stimulus (UCS)** that elicits an **unconditioned response (UCR),** that is, that reliably elicits an unlearned response, in the experimental subject. UCRs (unlearned responses) are also known as **reflexes.** The UCR is usually a physiological response that can reliably be elicited by a UCS, for example, salivation (the UCR) in response to the smell or sight of food (the UCS), particularly if one is hungry, or an eye blink (the UCR) in response to a puff of air (the UCS) blown into the eye. The classical conditioning procedure also requires a **conditioned stimulus (CS),** a stimulus of which the subject can be made aware but which initially does not cause the UCR, followed by a **conditioned response,** the same response as the UCR, but eventually in reaction to a different stimulus. For example, the CS in the puff of air example might be simply the sound of a buzzer, resulting, after conditioning is complete, in a blink (CR) caused by the CS alone.

Classical conditioning, then, would proceed as follows, using the four components and four steps.

- CS: The CS (conditioned stimulus)—for example, the sound of a buzzer— is presented in several trials.

- UCS: Each presentation of the CS is followed closely by presentation of the UCS (unconditioned stimulus)—for example, the puff of air.

- UCR: Presentation of the UCS causes a UCR (an eye blink).

- CR: After a sufficient number of presentations of the CS followed by the UCS, the experimenter presents the CS without the UCS. If a response, an eye blink, occurs, the UCR is now called a conditioned response (CR). The eye blink response to the buzzer has been conditioned (learned).

Shown graphically, the sequence is

CS (buzzer)→UCS (air puff)→UCR (eye blink)→CR (eye blink)

If the CS now produces a CR, with no presentation of the UCS, it can be said that conditioning (learning) has occurred and

CS (buzzer)→CR (eye blink)

Higher order conditioning. **Higher order conditioning,** that based upon previous learning, may also occur in the classical conditioning paradigm. In higher order conditioning, what was the CS comes to serve as a UCS. For example, if the experimenter always turned on a desk light before sounding the buzzer to begin classical conditioning (to produce an eye blink at the sound of the buzzer), the turning on of the light may eventually itself produce the eye blink, independent of the buzzer. In this case, the buzzer has become a UCS, and the turning on of the light has become a CS. Consequently, although initially

(light)→CS(buzzer)→UCS(air puff)→UCR(eye blink)→CR(eye blink)

higher order conditioning proceeds

CS (light)→UCS(buzzer)→UCR(eye blink)→CR(eye blink)

And higher order conditioning (learning) occurs:

CS (light)→CR (eye blink)

Classical conditioning terminology. Specific terminology is used to describe the classical conditioning procedure.

- The process of learning a conditioned response is called **acquisition.** Usually, conditioning is faster if only a short time elapses between the presentation of the CS and the UCS.

- The reverse process—that is, unlearning— can occur also and is called **extinction.** If the CS is presented for a time without the UCS, the CR will eventually cease (be **extinguished**).

- If the CS is again presented later, however, the CR will sometimes return temporarily (this temporary return is called **spontaneous recovery**). But the CR will disappear unless the UCS is at times reinstated.

Operant Conditioning

Operant conditioning is so named because the subject "operates" on the environment. An early theory of operant conditioning, proposed by Edward Thorndike, used the name **instrumental learning** because the response is "instrumental" in obtaining the reward. (Both operant and classical conditioning are also called **S-R learning** because a stimulus, S, has been paired with a response, R.)

A device called an **operant box** (sometimes called a **Skinner box**) was designed by the well-known experimenter B.F. Skinner. Learning in the operant conditioning procedure can be explained by the **law of effect** (also proposed by Thorndike, in 1911), which suggests that responses are learned when they are followed by a "satisfying state of affairs." Although operant conditioning requires the use of neither a CS nor a UCS, a CS can be employed but requires the use of shaping and reinforcement procedures.

Shaping. In operant conditioning, the subject must first *emit* the response that the experimenter plans to reward. Shaping is the name given to those initial steps needed to get the subject to engage in the behavior that is to be rewarded. If, for example, a rat is to be rewarded for pressing a bar, it must first learn

- to go near the bar in an operant box

- to touch the bar

- to press the bar

Generally, rewards (usually food) initially are given at the end of each of these steps. Finally, however, a reward is given only when the bar is pressed. (With subjects who understand spoken commands, shaping can sometimes be accomplished verbally.)

Positive and negative reinforcement. Reinforcement is the process of following an event with a second event meant to make the recurrence of the first event more likely. The second event itself is called the **reinforcer.**

Positive reinforcement is the presentation of a rewarding or *pleasant* stimulus (something that the subject wants, also called a **positive reinforcer**) that *increases* the probability that a particular response will occur. For example, if a student rewrites a term paper and is rewarded for that rewrite by a better grade, getting the grade is the positive reinforcer, and the teacher's awarding the grade to encourage rewrites is positive reinforcement. While a rat may learn to press a bar in an operant box if the action triggers a mechanism that delivers food, it may also respond to such rewards as water or even a minute amount of pleasurable electrical stimulation of a particular brain structure. (If food or water are to be used for reinforcement, the animal is usually first deprived of that substance for a time.)

Negative reinforcement, on the other hand, is the presentation of an *unpleasant* stimulus (something the subject does *not* want, also called a **negative reinforcer**) that *increases* the likelihood that a particular response, in order to remove or avoid the negative reinforcer, will occur. For example, giving a rat an unpleasant electric shock when it presses a bar increases the probability that the rat will avoid the bar-pressing action. As another example, a rat presented with such a negative reinforcer may learn to run to the right in a maze to avoid getting the shock that awaits it on the left, or a child may clean toys off the floor without being told in order to avoid a spanking (many of which were received in the past for not complying).

Punishment. Punishment differs from negative reinforcement in that it *decreases* the probability that a particular preceding event will occur again. When subjects are punished, they experience the unpleasant (aversive) stimulus rather than avoid it. Once experienced, punishment may sometimes serve as a negative reinforcer; a subject may increase certain types of responses to avoid the unpleasant experience. For example, a student who doesn't study may be punished by being given an *F* on an exam. But while the *F* was initially punishment, it can now serve as a negative reinforcer that causes the student to *increase* study time to avoid getting an *F*.

Schedule of reinforcement. Reinforcement can occur after every response, a situation called **continuous reinforcement.** It can also occur only after some responses, **intermittent reinforcement.** A response learned under the latter conditions is more resistant to extinction, a phenomenon called the **partial reinforcement effect.**

Psychologists have studied intermittent reinforcement effects by using various patterns of delivering rewards after a response. These patterns, called **schedules of reinforcement,** include

- **fixed-ratio schedule:** reinforcement after a set number of responses

- **variable-ratio schedule:** reinforcement after a variable number of responses

- **fixed-interval schedule:** reinforcement after the same (fixed) interval of time has elapsed

- **variable-interval schedule:** reinforcement after a variable interval of time has elapsed

The response styles of subjects, whether they be rats in operant boxes or employees in a workplace, vary based on the schedule used. Other things being equal, a variable-ratio schedule produces the most responses from a subject in a given time. A fixed-ratio schedule fosters quick learning of the desired response; the number of responses then remains steady but fewer than those produced by the variable-ratio schedule. Variable-interval schedules result in slower learning of the response followed by a steady number of responses (but fewer than those produced by the fixed-ratio schedule). Fixed-interval schedules produce both relatively few responses overall and a drop in number of responses right after reinforcement, although the number increases as the time for reinforcement nears. (It is interesting that most people are paid on a fixed-interval schedule. Perhaps productivity could be increased if more frequent rewards for good performance (bonuses) were given, that is, by using a fixed-ratio schedule.)

Primary and secondary reinforcers. In addition to being classified as positive or negative, reinforcers can be primary or secondary.

- A **primary reinforcer** is a substance (such as palatable food) or situation (such as the administration of a painful electric shock) that is universally rewarding or punishing.

- A **secondary reinforcer** is a formerly neutral stimulus that has acquired reward or punishment value, for example, the letters *A* or *F* given on examinations.

Stimulus Generalization

Stimulus generalization is the tendency of a subject to respond to a stimulus or a group of stimuli similar but not identical to the original CS. For example, a subject may initially make the desired response when exposed to any sound (that is, to a generalized stimulus) rather than making such a response only to a specific sound. Such generalization can occur in both classical and operant conditioning (if a CS is used). However, a subject can be taught to **discriminate** among sounds and to respond only to a specific sound.

Extinction

In operant conditioning, **extinction** (the cessation of a particular response) occurs when a response no longer results in reinforcement; it occurs in classical conditioning, as discussed earlier, when the CS no longer produces a CR. One way to measure the strength of the learning that has occurred (called **response strength**) is to see how many unreinforced trials must occur before extinction takes place, (called **resistance to extinction**). Sometimes, in both classical and operant conditioning, **spontaneous recovery** occurs; that is, the response in question begins again even though there has been no reinforcement (for example, a rat presses the bar even though the action no longer produces a food pellet).

Behavior Modification

The application of some of the principles of classical and operant conditioning to changing behavior is called **behavior modification.** Its major goal is to replace unacceptable responses with acceptable ones. Behavior modification is used in many situations, ranging from therapy to child rearing. Ignoring a child's temper tantrum but rewarding that child's polite behavior is an example of a behavior modification procedure. (For a discussion of the use of behavior modification in therapeutic situations, see p. 147.)

Contingency Theory

Contingency theorists argue that types of learning exist that are not explained by operant and classical conditioning. **Contingency theory** proposes that for learning to take place, a stimulus must provide the subject information about the likelihood that certain events will occur. Robert Rescorla demonstrated that the pairing of a CS and UCS does not always produce learning and contended that it is necessary for the CS to signify a **contingency.**

Learned helplessness. **Learned helplessness,** also demonstrated by Rescorla, results from situations in which no perceived connection (contingency) exists between a response and a reinforcer, suggesting to an individual that responses and outcomes are unrelated. When subjects' behavior has no effect upon reward, the result is apathy or unresponsiveness; they simply give up and no longer try. Martin Seligman also demonstrated that if individuals (both animal and human) believe they have no control in a situation, they exhibit learned helplessness, doing nothing and not trying to solve problems.

Cognitive Learning (S-S Learning)

Cognitive learning involves learning a relationship between two stimuli and thus is also called **S-S learning.** Types of cognitive learning include latent learning and the formation of insights.

Latent learning. **Latent learning** (sometimes called **incidental learning**) is learning without reinforcement and is not immediately demonstrated when it occurs. For example, if a student wants a coffee break, wonders where to go, and suddenly remembers a new coffee shop near campus, the student is demonstrating latent learning. E. C. Tolman, a well-known investigator of cognitive learning, suggested that organisms form **cognitive maps** of their environments, maps that can be used when needed.

Insight. An **insight** is a new way to organize stimuli or a new approach to solving a problem. A student struggling with a mathematical problem who suddenly sees how to solve it without having been taught additional methods has had an insight. Wolfgang Köhler, a famous Gestalt psychologist, demonstrated that chimpanzees can solve problems using insight. Chimps placed in a cage, with bananas beyond their reach, learned that they could pile up boxes or attach one stick to another to reach and obtain the food. The chimps had not been reinforced for these specific behaviors but learned how to get the food through insight. Once insight has occurred, no further instruction or training is required.

Social Learning Theory

Social learning theory proponents believe that much of our learning occurs through watching, often in social situations, what happens to other people.

Observational learning. **Observational learning,** sometimes called **modeling** or in some instances **vicarious learning,** is a type of social learning. In Albert Bandura's famous experiment, one group of nursery school children observed an adult punch a Bobo clown doll, and one group did not. Later, those children who had observed the punching behavior were more likely to punch the Bobo doll (model the adult's punching behavior) when they were frustrated than were those who had not observed it. Observational learning occurs also through exposure to events and people in the media. One may decide, for example, to copy the clothes or behaviors of television personalities. This tendency is one reason that many object to excessive violence in television programs both for children and for adults.

Factors That Influence Learning and Performance

It is important to distinguish between **learning** (including conditioning) and **performance.** The phenomena of cognitive maps and of latent learning both demonstrate that something may be learned but not shown until later.

Factors that influence learning. Several factors may affect learning.

- Learning generally increases with increased **amount of practice** or training. Practice alone, however, is not enough. Classical conditioning requires a UCS; operant conditioning requires reinforcement (positive or negative).

- Within limits, the **amount of reward** can affect learning, although the relationship between the two is complex, and the subject has been studied extensively. Surprisingly, an increase in reward can sometimes cause a decrease in response.

- **Delay of reward** is also much studied. In general, only a short time should elapse between a response and its reinforcement.

- In **partial reinforcement,** a subject is not rewarded every time for making a response. In general, partial reinforcement leads to a greater persistence in behavior than does continuous reinforcement. (Slot-machine players can attest to this fact.)

- **Interstimulus time,** the time between presentations of a given stimulus, can also be important in both classical and operant conditioning. Optimal conditions can be determined for a particular situation.

Factors that influence performance. Since learning is a relatively permanent change in behavior that occurs as a result of experience, experimenters must be certain that factors other than learning have not influenced the responses being studied and be alert to what those factors might be. Several factors that influence performance but not necessarily learning include the following.

- Variations in level of **motivation** can influence performance. For example, if two rats have been through the same conditioning process but one of them is denied food until it is very hungry, that rat may press a bar that produces a food pellet with more vigor than the less-hungry rat. The vigor of the response, in this case, does not reflect different degrees of learning—

both rats have learned the bar-pressing response—but rather different levels of motivation.

- **Stimulus intensity** may influence performance as well. But while a more intense CS might produce a stronger CR, the increased vigor of the response does not necessarily, and in general does not, indicate greater learning.

- If extreme **effort** must be used in a response, for example in pressing a weighted bar, fatigue may affect a subject's performance. **Intertrial intervals** have also been shown to affect performance. Too many trials too quickly can result in decreased performance simply because of fatigue or boredom.

Motivation, in an organism, is an inferred condition (that is, a **construct**—something inferred to exist and "constructed" from simpler, known elements) that arouses and directs it toward a specific goal. Motivational theories deal with and attempt to explain what instigates, directs, and maintains persistence in behavior. Many fields in psychology are concerned with motivation, and its study is approached from various perspectives, including the biological/physiological, the behavioral, the cognitive, and that based on a need hierarchy.

The Biological/Physiological Perspective

Biological/physiological approaches to motivation evolved from the work of Charles Darwin, who was interested in evolution and how species survived.

Instincts. Darwin explained survival of an organism, and consequently a species, as, in part, resulting from an **instinct for survival.** Other early attempts to explain motivation (by, for example, William James and William McDougall) also involved **instincts,** defined by some as unlearned patterns of behavior that aid in the survival of the organism. Explaining behavior in terms of instincts eventually fell out of favor, however, because of the indiscriminate labeling of all motivated behaviors as instincts (till they reached the thousands and included such things as instincts for rivalry, cleanliness, or parental love).

Ethology. Ethology, a branch of biology that studies evolution and the development and function of behavior, emerged in the 1930s and revived interest in instincts. Early theorists in the field include Konrad Lorenz, Nikolaas Tinbergen, and Irenaus Eibl-Eibesfeldt. (Eibl-

Eibesfeldt investigated the possibility that certain human behaviors are universal, such as the display of facial expressions to express happiness or sadness.) The term instinct, as used by these theorists, has to do with unlearned behaviors and responses (for example, Tinbergen spoke of the reproductive instinct). Ethological theory became controversial, partly because it initially excluded certain known facts concerning nervous system functions and their effects on behavior. Although other approaches are now used more widely in the study of human motivation, ethology is still important in the study of animal behavior.

Sociobiology. Sociobiology, a contemporary discipline that evolved from instinct theories, is the study of the evolutionary and genetic foundations of social behavior in all species. Although the discipline is not universally accepted and its concepts have often been controversial because of the difficulty of verifying them through experimentation, sociobiology remains an active area of study.

Physiological regulation. In motivation theory, **physiological regulation** refers to the regulation of motivation by certain portions of the nervous system. Particular origins of such regulatory activity are proposed in what are known as local theories and central theories.

- **Local theories** suggest that signals that regulate motivation come from the peripheral organs of the body (as opposed to the brain). But popular work (such as that by Walter Cannon and A. L. Washburn) in the early 1900s demonstrated that although the experience of hunger is related to hunger pangs (stomach activity), when the vagus nerve is severed, eliminating stomach contractions, hunger is still experienced. Such work led to decreased interest in local theories of regulation and subsequent focus on central regulation.

- **Central theories** describe regulation of motivation by the brain, particularly by the hypothalamus. Motivations arising from hunger, thirst, and sexual appetite have been studied extensively from the central theory perspective.

Physiological regulation includes both short-term and long-term regulatory mechanisms.

- **Short-term regulation** refers to immediate physiological changes, such as those in blood-sugar level when one eats.

- **Long-term regulation** refers to central nervous system mechanisms that function to maintain a steady state of physiological functioning, for example, maintenance of a relatively stable body weight. These regulatory systems are described in more detail in the following discussion of hunger, thirst, and sexual motivation

Hunger

Hunger regulation. Hunger is now known to be regulated on **a short-term basis** by two clusters of cells (called **nuclei**) in the hypothalamus of the brain, the **ventromedial hypothalamic (VMH)** and the **lateral hypothalamic (LH) nuclei** (Figure 13).

The Hypothalamic Nuclei

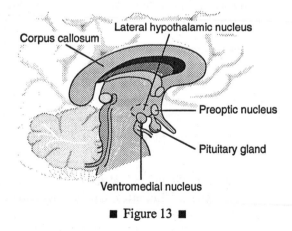

■ Figure 13 ■

Lesioning (destruction) produces effects on motivated behavior that are opposite those produced by electrical stimulation of the same nucleus. Damage to a rat's LH causes the rat to stop eating (become aphagic) and eventually starve to death even with an abundance of food. Electrical stimulation of the LH, however, causes it to eat. Conversely, damage to a rat's VMH causes it to overeat (become hyperphagic). (If an adult female rat of a species weighs 350 grams, a hyperphagic rat of the same species can weigh over 1,000 grams.) Electrical stimulation in the same VMH nucleus produces cessation of eating.

Long-term regulation of hunger is less understood, but one theory, the **set-point theory,** suggests that the body has a weight regulatory system, which establishes a "set-point" that regulates body weight on a long-term basis. This theory could explain, for example, why a hyperphagic rat, even though very overweight, finally stops eating. While the set-point mechanism is not known, one view is that the regulation includes an interaction with the level of body fat. If body fat increases, eating is less frequent and activity increases; the converse is true if body fat decreases.

Other changes can also affect hunger, such as changes in glucose (blood sugar) and hormone levels. For example, the hormone insulin diminishes the blood glucose level, producing hunger and thus increasing eating behavior. In addition, external cues may affect eating behavior, for example, the sight or aroma of food or the sight of other people eating.

Eating disorders. Theoretical explanations of eating behavior are still being explored, particularly with the increasing occurrence of eating disorders such as anorexia nervosa and bulimia nervosa. (The majority of individuals with eating disorders are female, a phenomenon possibly explained by society's expectations that the ideal female must be very thin.)

In **anorexia nervosa,** the individual suffers starvation caused by repeated calorie restriction. Ultimately, the disorder can be fatal (as it was for singer Karen Carpenter). A person afflicted with **bulimia nervosa** goes on eating binges and then purges, inducing vomiting or using laxatives, to get rid of the ingested food. This behavior also is ultimately detrimental to health. **Obesity,** another failure of hunger regulation, is found in individuals of all ages and genders.

Thirst

Thirst motivation, like that of hunger, is regulated by peripheral and central nervous system mechanisms. In part, thirst regulation involves

- both the intra- and extra-cellular water content of the cells in the body
- a chemical (**angiotensin**) produced by the kidneys
- a hormone (**antidiuretic hormone (ADH)**, also called **vasopressin**) produced by the pituitary gland

Central nervous system structures such as the **subfornical organ** and the **LH (lateral hypothalamic nucleus)** also help regulate thirst. Damage to the LH causes the animal to become **adipsic** (fail to drink) as well as to become aphagic (fail to eat). The **double depletion hypothesis** contends that thirst is produced by depletion of fluid both outside and within cells.

Sexual Motivation

Sexual repsonse regulation. Level of **sexual motivation,** as well as that of thirst and hunger, can be changed by damage to or stimulation of certain areas of the hypothalamus (including the **medial preoptic area** and the **VMH**) (Figure 13) and other portions of the brain (such as the limbic system). Sexual behavior is also affected by levels of the sexual hormones—primarily, testosterone in males and estrogens in females—produced by the gonads. Sexual hormone production in the gonads is, in turn, controlled by hormones produced in the pituitary gland. Sexual behavior is complex, however, and may be affected by many factors, particularly during development, such as administration of sex hormones or ingestion of drugs that affect production of sex hormones.

The sexual response cycle. William Masters and Virginia Johnson described the **sexual response cycle** in both females and males as comprising four phases:

- **excitement:** initial arousal of genital areas

- **plateau:** continued excitement, increasing rates of breathing and pulse, and increasing blood pressure

- **orgasm:** rapid contraction of muscles in genital area, release of semen by male, feeling of pleasure by both genders

- **resolution:** return of body to an unaroused state

Sexual dysfunction. Some individuals experience difficulties in one or more of the sexual response phases. Such problems and other **sexual dysfunctions** are of concern to those psychologists working with behavior problems. Problems include, among others, **premature ejaculation** and **impotence** (inability to be physically aroused) in males and inability to experience orgasms (**organismic dysfunction**) and low sexual desire in females.

Sexual orientation. Sexual orientation refers to the direction of one's erotic interests. **Heterosexuals** are attracted to people of the opposite gender; **homosexuals** (gay males and **lesbian** females) are attracted to people of the same gender; **bisexuals** are attracted to members of either gender. Differences in sexual orientation exist in all cultures. Most psychologists today tend to view sexual orientation as a characteristic of human behavior that is neither willfully chosen nor willfully changed; people are born one way or another. A 1996 survey found that 3.5% of the men and 2.1 % of the women reported having had a homosexual experience within the past 12 months. Sexual orientation is not linked to any type of psychological disorder or sexual crime (such as child molestation). Homosexuality was dropped as a "mental illness" by the American Psychiatric Association in 1973.

Electrical Stimulation of the Brain (ESB)

In 1954, James Olds and Peter Milner discovered that a rat would press a bar to receive a brief impulse of electricity through an electrode implanted in certain areas of the brain. Although it was known that such stimulation in other areas of the brain could produce motivated behaviors of eating, drinking, sexual behavior, or aggression (and that lesions of the brain could produce the converse behaviors), it now appeared that psychologists had discovered a "brain reward" system. The ESB was serving as a reinforcer. Rats bar pressed at rapid rates for 15 to 20 hours until exhausted in order to receive the stimulation. During the process, they ignored food or water, and rat mothers ignored their pups. Jose Delgado, in 1955, demonstrated that rats would also learn to bar press in order to turn off stimulation to the hippocampus, a neural system not involved in pain transmission. Other researchers found that the positive and negative ESB sites (stimulation of which induced animals to obtain or avoid receiving ESB) appeared to be concentrated in the limbic system.

Humans who have had electrodes implanted in their brains to alleviate symptoms of Parkinson's disease have described the experience as mildly pleasurable and satisfying. Although ESB has been found to result in the release of neurotransmitters such as dopamine and norepinephrine, current research strategies have focused on the use of drugs rather than ESB to regulate production of these neurotransmitters.

The Behavioral Perspective

The **behavioral** approach to understanding motivation deals with drives, both learned and unlearned, and with incentives.

Drive theory. **Drive theory** involves the concepts of unlearned (or primary) drives, drive reduction, and learned (secondary) drives. It is based on the fact that all living organisms have **physiological needs** that must be satisfied for survival (for example, the need for food, water, sleep, and so forth) to maintain a state of **homeostasis,** that is, a steady internal state.

Disruption of an organism's homeostatic state causes a state of tension (arousal) called an **unlearned,** or **primary, drive.** If the aroused state has been created by hunger, it is called a **hunger drive,** and the drive can be *reduced* by food. Drive reduction moves toward the re-establishment of homeostasis. Drives, then, may be thought of as the consequence of a physiological need, which an organism is impelled to reduce or eliminate. Clark Hull, a learning theorist, developed an equation to show how learning and drive are related.

Drives may also be **learned,** or **secondary.** Fear (or anxiety), for example, is often considered a secondary drive that can be learned through either classical or operant conditioning. In Neal Miller's well-known operant conditioning experiment, a rat was placed in a black box and then given a mild electrical shock. Eventually, the rat learned to react to the experience of being put in a black box (with no shock given) with the response of turning a wheel to escape. In this case, the black box is said to have elicited the learned drive of fear. Among other drives considered by some theorists to be learned are the need for affiliation (that is, to belong, to have companionship), the need for security (money), and the need for achievement.

Incentive motivation. Theories of **incentive motivation** contend that **external stimuli** can motivate behavior. Humans (and other animals) can learn to value external stimuli (for example, the first prize in a track meet for a human and a pat on the head for a dog) and will work to get them. Incentive motivation is sometimes called "pull" motivation because incentives are said to "pull" in contrast with the "push" associated with drives.

Kenneth Spence, well known for his work in incentive motivation, suggested that the incentive value of the reward strengthens the response. (One would run faster for a reward of $100 than for one of $1.)

The Cognitive Perspective

Cognitive behavior represents another approach to understanding the effects of learning on the instigation of behavior. In the process of learning that particular behaviors can lead to particular goals, expectations about the goals are established and the goals acquire values. One **cognitive** approach to motivation, called **expectancy-value theory,** stresses that the probability of occurrence of behavior depends upon individuals' perception of the value of a goal as well as their expectation of reaching it. Variations of the theory have been used to study such motives as the need for **achievement** (Henry Murray) and the need for **success** (John Atkinson).

Other cognitive motivational theories focus on individual characteristics and how those characteristics relate to motivation. Carl Rogers, for example, proposed that an individual strives to become **self-actualized,** a process important in the development of a mature personality. (See p. 127.)

The Need Hierarchy

Some theories incorporate more than one type of motive. Abraham Maslow developed a motivational theory that includes both physiological and cognitive motives ranked in a hierarchy from basic to higher level. According to Maslow, individuals must first meet the most basic needs—that is, physiological survival needs—before they can attend to those of higher levels. Maslow, like Rogers, was concerned with individuals' self-actualization, their achievement of the highest level of development The order of needs from highest (1) to lowest (7) is

1. need for self-actualization

2. aesthetic needs

3. cognitive needs

4. esteem needs

5. belongingness and love needs

6. safety and security needs

7. physiological needs

Emotion is complex, and the term has no single universally accepted definition. Emotion is, however, closely related to motivation and can sometimes provide motivation (as, for example, a student's fear of failing provides motivation for studying). Psychologists do agree that emotions are reaction patterns that include

- physiological changes
- responses or goal-oriented behaviors
- affective experiences (feelings)

Theorists differ on the order of appearance of the reaction patterns.

Biological/Physiological Factors in Emotion

The autonomic nervous system. The **autonomic nervous system (ANS)** has two components, the **sympathetic nervous system (SNS)** and the **parasympathetic nervous system (PNS)**. (See Figure 4, p. 23.) When activated, the SNS prepares the body for emergency actions; it controls glands of the neuroendocrine system (thyroid, pituitary, and adrenal glands). Activation of the SNS causes the production of **epinephrine** (adrenaline) from the adrenal glands, increased blood flow to the muscles, increased heart rate, and other readiness reactions. Conversely, the PNS functions when the body is relaxed or at rest and helps the body store energy for future use. PNS effects include increased stomach activity and decreased blood flow to the muscles.

The reticular activating system. The **reticular activating system (RAS)** is a network of neurons that runs through the core of the hindbrain and into the midbrain and forebrain. It has been demonstrated that electrical stimulation of the RAS causes changes in the electrical activity of the cortex (as measured by an electroencephalogram) that are indistinguishable from changes in electrical activity seen when external stimuli (such as loud sounds) are present. The **RAS** is believed to first arouse the cortex and then to stimulate its wakefulness so that it may more effectively interpret sensory information.

The limbic system. The **limbic system** includes the **anterior thalamus,** the **amygdala,** the **septal area,** the **hippocampus,** the **cingulate gyrus,** and structures that are parts of the hypothalamus (Figure 14). The word *limbic* means "border" and describes this system because its structures seem to form a rough border along the inner edge of the cerebrum. Studies have associated the limbic system with such emotions as fear and aggression as well with as drives, including those for food and sex.

The Limbic System

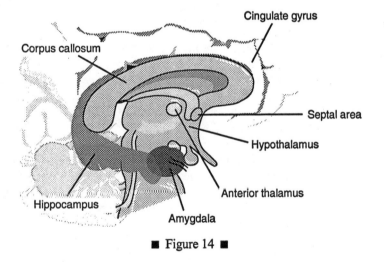

■ Figure 14 ■

Lie detectors (polygraphs). **Lie detectors,** or **polygraphs,** rely upon the physiological arousal of the emotions. Concomitant measurements are taken of the heart rate, blood pressure, respiration rate, and **galvanic skin response (GSR).** (The GSR is a measure of the skin's electrical conductivity, which changes as the sweat glands increase their activity.) Polygraph recordings are used to see if a person is not telling the truth (lying), which usually creates emotional arousal. Because of polygraphs' high error rates, however, their findings are generally not accepted as evidence in the courts.

Early Theories of Emotion

Darwin. Darwin believed that body movements and facial expressions (body language, or nonverbal communication) are used by members of a species to communicate meaning. He suggested that although emotional expressions are initially learned behavior, they eventually evolve to become innate in a species because they have survival value. Recognition by one animal that a second animal is afraid rather than angry, for example, allows appropriate survival actions to be undertaken.

The James-Lange theory. Two theorists, William James in 1884 and Carl Lange in 1885, independently proposed that emotions do not immediately follow the perception of an event but rather occur after the body has responded to the event. Their ideas were combined into the **James-Lange theory of emotion.** According to the theory, the perception of an environmental stimulus (such as a growling dog) causes bodily changes (such as rapid heart beat and fast breathing). The brain perceives those changes in behavior and identifies them as the emotion. The progression is

A dog is growling.
stimulus

↓

My heart is beating fast. I'm breathing hard.
perception of physiological changes

↓

Therefore, I am afraid.
identification of emotion

The Cannon-Bard theory. Walter Cannon criticized the James-Lange theory for several reasons. He argued that emotion occurs even if the bodily changes which transmit feedback to the brain are eliminated. He severed neural connections to the cortex of cats (creating "decorticate cats"). The decorticate cats, when provoked, exhibited the emotional behavior normally associated with rage and aggression, as demonstrated by erect hair, growling, and the baring of teeth. (Canon called the behavior **sham rage** because according to the James-Lange theory emotional behavior could not occur without connections to the brain.) In addition, Cannon argued that visceral responses occur too slowly to be recognized by the brain before emotional responses to a stimuli occur.

Philip Bard agreed with Cannon and expanded on his work in what is now known as the **Cannon-Bard theory** (also called the **emergency theory**), which argues that the **thalamus,** a lower brain stem structure (part of the limbic system) is necessary for emotional responses. The thalamus sends messages to the cortex for interpretation of the emotion and simultaneously to the sympathetic nervous system for appropriate physical responses. According to the Cannon-Bard theory, then, the identification (experience) of an emotion occurs at the same time as the activation of bodily responses and not because of them (as the James-Lange theory proposed). The progression is

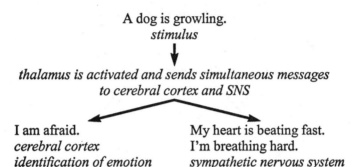

A dog is growling.
stimulus

thalamus is activated and sends simultaneous messages to cerebral cortex and SNS

I am afraid.
cerebral cortex
identification of emotion

My heart is beating fast.
I'm breathing hard.
sympathetic nervous system
bodily changes

The Schachter-Singer theory. Stanley Schachter and Jerome Singer proposed that experiencing an emotion requires both **emotional arousal** and **cognitive activity** (perception, reasoning, memory) to understand the reason for the arousal (that is, to appraise the stimuli) so that the emotion can then be appropriately identified. (The process of labeling the stimuli producing an emotion is called **attribution.**) Schachter and Singer concluded that although individuals usually are aware of the reason for their aroused emotional state, if the reason is not apparent, they search their environment for clues to help them interpret the emotion. Although this theory has generated a great deal of research, experimental data only partially support it.

Arousal theory. Many researchers propose that behavior changes as a function of arousal. The curve (called an **inverted U function**) shown in Figure 15 illustrates that performance increases as arousal increases up to a point but then decreases if arousal is increased beyond that point. This arousal-performance phenomenon is known as the **Yerkes-Dodson law.** It is well known that while a certain amount of anxiety can enhance performance (for example, by promoting thorough preparation), too much can impair it (as could, for example, severe stage fright). Research evidence has not totally supported the inverted U relationship for all types of tasks, particularly those that are complex.

The Inverted U Function

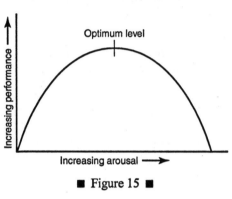

■ Figure 15 ■

Learning Factors in Emotion

Emotions may also be learned. For example, fear may be learned through **conditioning** (p. 61), and once fear is learned, the drive to avoid it is a powerful motivator. The learning of some fears, however, as well as certain other emotions, may involve other processes, which are discussed later.

Emotional responses may be learned also through **modeling.** The high incidence of violence in our society is seen by some to be related to the high incidence of violence in the media, particularly television and movies. (See the discussion of the study by Bandura, p. 68.)

Cognitive Factors in Emotion

Other reasearchers, as well as Schachter and Singer, have constructed **attribution** theories of emotion (concerning the using of external clues to identify a particular emotion). For example, in a study by Stuart Valins, as male subjects were shown pictures of seminude females, they heard amplified heartbeats that they were told were theirs (although they were not) and that varied in rate. The subjects attributed their varying heart rates to the varying pictures they were shown and picked pictures they believed produced their most rapid heart rate as being the most attractive. (This approach has been applied in some therapeutic treatments of people suffering from delusions.)

Other Theories of Emotion

The circumplex theory. J. A. Russell and H. Schlosberg, in what is called the **circumplex theory of emotion,** proposed that there are two essential dimensions (axes) of emotions, pleasantness versus misery and arousal versus sleepiness (Figure 16). The names of various emotions, they suggested, could then be arranged in a circular fashion around these axes, with the placement indicating the relationship of emotions to one another. Excitement, for example, would lie in the quadrant bounded by arousal and pleasure, whereas distress would be in the quadrant bounded by misery and arousal.

Axes of Emotions

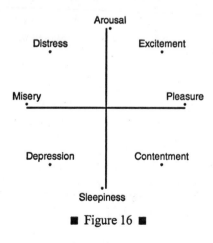

■ Figure 16 ■

Tomkins's theory. Silvan Tomkins suggested that human emotions are of a limited number, genetically preprogrammed into the brain, and triggered by changes in stimulation. Changes in stimulation produce changes in patterns of neural firing that, in turn, cause changes in emotional experiences. According to Tomkins, emotion intensifies motivation and is necessary to instigate behavior. He proposed also that a preprogrammed set of facial-muscle responses and vocalizations are associated with each emotion and allow the communication of emotional states.

Izard's theory. Carroll Izard identified ten primary emotions: fear, anger, shame, contempt, disgust, guilt, distress, interest, surprise, and joy—emotions that cannot be reduced to more basic emotions but that can be combined to produce other emotions. He further suggested that each emotion has its own neural basis and pattern of expression (usually denoted by facial expressions) and that each is experienced uniquely.

Plutchik's theory. Robert Plutchik argued for eight primary emotions, each directly related to an adaptive pattern of behavior necessary for survival. The eight emotions are anger, fear, sadness, disgust, surprise, expectancy, acceptance, and joy. Plutchik suggested that other emotions are variations of these eight and that emotions can complexly combine and can vary in intensity and persistence.

The opponent-process theory. The **opponent-process theory,** proposed by Richard Solomon and John Corbit, suggests that the experiencing of emotions disrupts the body's state of **homeostasis** and that emotions occur in basically opposite pairs—pleasure-pain, depression-elation, fear-relief, and so forth—and oppose one another so that homeostasis can once again be achieved. The theory suggests that the experiencing of one emotion of a pair prompts the onset of the other emotion (the opponent process) as well, which eventually reduces the intensity of the first emotion and finally cancels it out. For example, although a rock climber may be terrified (an unpleasant emotion) in several climbs of a steep cliff, eventually, the thrill of safely reaching the top (a pleasant emotion) will cancel out that early fear. Some psychologists use this theory to explain drug addiction. The pleasure associated with taking an addictive drug is said to decrease over time because an opponent process is operating to reduce the pleasure. Consequently, more and more of the drug must be taken to achieve the original euphoric state and to avoid the pain of withdrawal.

Nonverbal Communication of Emotion

Ethologists (see p. 71) have studied the way in which information is conveyed by **intention movements** that accompany the expression of emotions. When a dog bares its teeth or wags its tail, it communicates its likely subsequent actions, communication which both humans and other species understand. Such communications are adaptive and allow members of a species to live in close proximity and to interact efficiently. Ethologists also believe that primates, including humans, use **nonverbal cues** (facial expressions, gestures, sounds) to indicate emotional states. Movement such as crossing the arms, lowering the head, and standing rigidly, for example, can communicate in **body language** a negative attitude. Researchers have also been interested in the universality of particular facial expressions as indicators of particular emotions, and some do indeed seem to be universal. But some facial expressions and other gestures differ in meaning from culture to culture and are regulated by cultural norms called **display rules.**

Stress may be defined as a nonspecific response to perceived environmental threats (called **stressors**). But a particular environmental change (a demand or an event) may be perceived by one person as stressful and by another as benign. An examination is, for example, likely to be less stressful for a student who has mastered all homework assignments than it is for a student who waits to cram the night before the test. The generalized feeling of fear and apprehension associated with a stressor is called **anxiety.** Anxiety is typically accompanied by activation of the sympathetic nervous system and increased physiological arousal, which causes rapid breathing, increased heart rate, sweating, and dilation of the pupils.

Stress Response Theories

Fight or flight. In the 1920s, Walter Cannon recognized that the autonomic nervous system is activated in response to stress and suggested that stress mobilizes the body's responses in readiness for either attacking (**fight**) or fleeing (**flight**) an enemy or threatening situation. Although such responses may have promoted survival when they evolved in human history, they are not productive given the longer periods of stress exposure common in modern life. Such enterprises as keeping a job, going to school, and playing on the soccer team require more complex responses.

The general adaptation syndrome. Hans Selye is credited with identifying the body's reaction to stress with a syndrome he called the **general adaptation syndrome,** which has three phases, as evidenced by the level of stress hormones (Figure 17).

- **alarm:** The body first organizes physiological responses (similar to fight-or-flight responses) to threat.

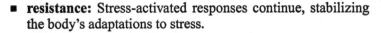

- **resistance:** Stress-activated responses continue, stabilizing the body's adaptations to stress.

- **exhaustion:** The body has depleted its reserves and can no longer maintain responses to the stressors.

The General Adaptation Syndrome

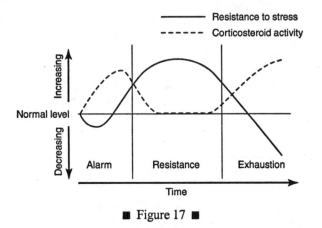

■ Figure 17 ■

During the alarm phase, when the body is first aroused, the hypothalamus sends signals to the pituitary gland. This endocrine gland in turn secretes **adrenocorticotrophic hormone (ACTH)**, which travels via the bloodstream to the cortex (outer layer) of the adrenal glands, where **corticosteroids** are released. The hypothalamus also activates the adrenal medulla, the central part of the adrenal gland, which causes **adrenaline (epinephrine)** to be released and the activation of the sympathetic nervous system. After maintaining high levels of the hormones for a long time, the body loses its ability to do so and exhausts its resources. Selye is credited with identifying the fact that the incidence of certain types of diseases (**stress-related diseases,** such as some types of coronary disorders) increases during this stage of exhausted body resources and that a second stressor introduced during the resistance phase or the exhaustion phase further increases that incidence.

Evidence demonstrates that prolonged stress also affects the ability of the immune system to function adequately and can affect the release of other neurotransmitters such as serotonin. Stress may also affect the release of **endorphins,** chemicals similar in structure to morphine and other opiate drugs used in the modulation of pain.

The Origins of Stress

The origins of stress may vary with the individual, but in general, stress arises from frustration, life changes, conflict, lack of control, and uncertainty.

Frustration. Frustration occurs when an individual is blocked or thwarted, whether by personal or environmental factors, in an attempt to reach a goal. **Personal frustration** and accompanying stress could result, for example, if an individual who lacks adequate vocal skills repeatedly tries out for (perhaps because of parental pressure) but fails to be accepted by a glee club. If such attempts are too intense or too prolonged, the stress can provoke bodily symptoms and illness. **Environmental frustration** and accompanying stress could result, for example, if an individual auditioning for a glee club has to deal with unfamiliar music, a poorly prepared accompanist, loud noises, or some other environmental annoyance.

Frustration can motivate **aggression.** Experiment subjects (including humans, pigeons, monkeys, and rats) show an inclination to attack if they do not receive expected rewards, although aggression is less likely if other responses to frustration have been learned. Experimentally, it has also been shown that **increased response vigor** may occur in response to frustrating circumstances. If increased vigor does not produce desired results, a subject may then react with **escape** or **avoidance** responses. If these responses are not possible, a subject may enter, after prolonged frustration, into a psychological state of **depression.**

Life changes. Life changes, both those perceived as "good" (such as marriage or the birth of a baby) or as "bad" (such as the death of a parent, a tragic accident, or being fired) can produce stress and stress-related responses. Thomas Holmes and Richard Rahe in 1967 developed the **Social Readjustment Rating Scale,** which assigns numerical values to 43 life events ranging from "death of spouse" (100 points) to "minor violations of the law" (11 points). A subject checks the events that have occurred within a particular period of time, and the point total provides an index of **life-change stress.** Although some research supports the efficacy of the scale, more recent research has indicated that other factors may moderate the impact of the stressful event and that these situations may be assessed differently by different individuals.

Conflict. Conflict occurs when two incompatible goals or possible behavioral responses are simultaneously present. When conflicts are unresolved, they cause stress. Neal Miller, in a detailed analysis of the types of conflicts and strategies for resolving them, identified approach-approach, avoidance-avoidance, and approach-avoidance conflicts.

- An **approach-approach conflict** occurs when an individual must choose between two equally desirable goals, such as either chocolate cake or apple pie for dessert. These conflicts are usually the easiest to resolve.

- An **avoidance-avoidance conflict** occurs when an individual must choose between two equally undesirable goals or activities. A child who is dared to climb a flagpole and is afraid of being called a coward if the dare is refused but is also afraid of falling if the climb is attempted is faced with an avoidance-avoidance conflict.

- An **approach-avoidance conflict** is the result of having concomitant but incompatible goals. Such would be the case when a student wants to do well on an exam but also wants to spend the evening watching television instead of studying.

The three types of conflicts can be depicted graphically as gradients of response strengths for approach and avoidance. Typically, the strength of the tendency to avoid or approach increases as one nears the goal. Where the gradients intersect, conflict occurs. Experimentally, response-strength gradients have been constructed by measuring how hard rats pull, at various distances from a goal, to approach the goal or to retreat from it.

Approach-avoidance conflicts (Figure 18) lead to indecisiveness. Experimentally, it has been shown that avoidance responses become more dominant the closer one comes to a goal that has both positive and negative aspects, causing one to retreat from the goal to a point at which strength of the approach and avoidance responses are in balance (causing the indecisiveness). Retreat may also proceed far enough that approach may once again be attempted. A method for resolving an approach-avoidance conflict is to change the strength of one of the conflicting motives so that they are not equal (that is, so that the strength of the tendency to approach is stronger).

An Approach-Avoidance Conflict

■ Figure 18 ■

Lack of control and uncertainty. Studies have demonstrated that elderly people in nursing homes who exert some **control** over their placement in such facilities and over their daily activities have less stress and better health. Animal studies have shown that **uncertainty** of the occurrence of an aversive event increases its aversiveness.

Effects of Stress

Impaired performance. Impaired performance, the inability to handle effectively a task at hand, can be a consequence of stress. For example, a student called to the front of the class to demonstrate a geometry theorem on the chalkboard may be embarrassed and not do as well as when working alone.

Burnout. Stress can sometimes result in the complete mental and physical exhaustion called **burnout.** The emotional state that accompanies it often includes feelings of being trapped, hopeless, and helpless.

Psychosomatic disorders. Psychosomatic disorders are physical disorders that appear to result from prolonged exposure to psychological conflict. Disorders such as peptic ulcers, asthma, hypertension, chronic headaches, and some types of menstrual problems are sometimes classed as stress-related.

Posttraumatic stress disorder (PTSD). The effects of stress may not always be immediately apparent but may occur some time after the stress has been removed, as happened with many veterans of the Vietnam War. Symptoms included sleep disturbances, paranoia, emotional numbing, guilt about surviving the war, alienation, and difficulties with social relationships.

Other stress-related problems. Other problems associated with stress include drug abuse, sexual difficulties, sleep disturbances, eating disorders, and poor academic performance. Stress also plays a role in major psychological disorders such as depression, some psychoses, and some neuroses.

Personality Factors and Stress

The Type A personality. Two California cardiologists, Meyer Friedman and Ray Rosenman, observed differences in patterns of behavior of their cardiac patients, differences they related to types of cardiac problems. One group was identified as possessing a **Type A behavior pattern,** which is characterized by excessively competitive, hard-driven, achievement-oriented, impatient, and sometimes hostile behaviors. The Type A individual is described as being easily aroused, very concerned over wasting time, and often angry. Beginning in the 1980s, health care professionals sought to identify these individuals in order to intervene and prevent the development of coronary problems. Subsequent studies, however, have not universally supported the concept, and researchers argue that more research is needed in order to correctly identify these coronary-disease-prone individuals.

Hardiness. A personality factor called **hardiness** was also identified in psychological studies of health issues. Over time, male business executives were studied, and those in the group who most adequately survived stressful events were said to have a **hardy** personality style and to be characterized by

- **commitment:** devotion to jobs, families, and other valued activities

- **control:** a sense of personal mastery over their activities and lives

- **challenge:** a perception of life events as challenging (not threatening) and as an opportunity to test themselves

Other studies have found that while commitment and control are associated with good health, challenge is not always necessary. However, feeling helpless (that is, not in control) and being uncommitted have themselves been found to be stressful conditions, and people with an optimistic outlook on life have been found to be healthier.

Health-Related Disciplines

Stress is a main area of research in both behavioral medicine and health psychology, and both disciplines have developed techniques to identify and deal with stress-related problems.

Behavioral medicine. The relationship between stress and disease has led many health care professionals to become interested in ways that behavior could be modified and psychological information used to improve health. The interdisciplinary field of **behavioral medicine** attempts to combine medical and behavioral knowledge in that endeavor.

Health psychology. The discipline of **health psychology** focuses on promoting good health and health care and investigates psychological and social factors important in preventing and treating illness. Health care psychologists are interested in reasons people do (or do not) comply with medical advice or act on information concerning maintenance of good health (losing weight, stopping smoking, regularly exercising, and so forth). Many habits, personality traits, and stressful situations, when identified, may be modified to reduce health risks. Health psychologists participate both in the identification of stress and in **stress-modification** procedures.

Coping with Stress

Direct action. One stress-reducing tactic is facing a problem directly by identifying it and then developing a strategy to solve it. For example, for students who become highly anxious at exam times, recognizing that their studying has not been adequate and developing more efficient class-preparation procedures can be helpful.

Aerobic exercise. Aerobic exercise has been shown to be useful in stress reduction. People must be sure, of course, to choose exercise programs appropriate for their general health and strength.

Relaxation. Relaxation strategies, which can effectively alleviate stress, vary widely and range from programs of **progressive relaxation** and **relaxation therapy** to short-term techniques such as taking a minute or two to breathe deeply and count, providing a momentary escape from a stressful situation.

Social support. Social support from friends and relatives is helpful in dealing with stressful situations. Gathering of friends and relatives at a funeral, for instance, is supportive and stress relieving for the person dealing with such exceedingly difficult, if universal, circumstances.

Biofeedback. Teaching a subject to use **biofeedback** is process of operant conditioning that is used to change physiological responses such as abnormal heart rate or blood pressure by associating external cues with these responses. For example, a subject's heart rate may be monitored and a tone sounded, progressively louder as the rate increases and softer as it decreases. The subject eventually learns to recognize the level of and to some degree regulate the heart rate without benefit of the sound.

Developmental **psychology** is concerned with both physical and psychological changes throughout life—from conception until death. Although theorists differ in their identification of developmental stages and the ages at which they occur, the breakdown is usually similar to that shown in Table 3.

STAGES IN LIFE	
Life Stage	**Approximate Age**
Prenatal stage	
Conception	Formation of zygote
Germinal	Conception–week 2
Embryo	Week 2–week 8
Fetus	Week 8–birth
Postnatal stage	
Infancy	Birth–2 years
Toddler	2–3 years
Early childhood	3–6 years
Middle childhood	6–13 years
Adolescence	13–20 years
Young adulthood	20–40 years
Middle adulthood	40–65 years
Late adulthood	65+ years

 ■ Table 3 ■

Nature and Nurture

The relative contributions of **nature** (genetic and biological inheritance) and **nurture** (environmental factors) in developmental processes has been and continues to be debated. Psychologists investigate, by using both longitudinal and cross-sectional studies of subjects in each developmental period, how both nature and nurture influence behavior.

When put together, the study data provide information about changes over the entire life span.

Identical twins are often studied in nature-nurture investigations (because identical twins develop from one egg, but fraternal twins develop from separate eggs and are genetically no more similar than are any brothers or sisters). Studies have shown that identical twins are more similar in personalities, abilities, and interests than are other siblings, even those identical twins separated at birth and reared apart, a fact that supports the contention that nature (heredity) may be more developmentally important than nurture.

Prenatal Development

The **prenatal development** period covers the time from conception to birth and is sometimes described in terms of trimesters (first, second, and third) or of three stages (germinal, embryonic, and fetal).

Conception. **Conception,** which occurs when the father's sperm cell penetrates the mother's ovum (egg), marks the beginning of development. The sperm cell/ovum combination creates a **zygote,** a one-celled organism. All other cells in the body develop from this single cell. Each sperm and each egg cell carry 23 **chromosomes,** threadlike chains of DNA (deoxyribonucleic acid) that carry genetic information, which unite during fertilization to form 23 pairs of chromosomes. **Genes** are DNA segments that are functional units in hereditary transmission. After conception, all body cells except **gametes** (eggs or sperm) contain 23 pairs of chromosomes. The gender of the offspring is determined by the type of sex chromosome in the sperm that fertilizes the ovum; if it is Y bearing, the offspring will be male, and if it is X bearing, the offspring will be female.

The germinal stage. The **germinal stage** extends from conception to two weeks. During this period, the cells in the zygote divide rapidly, and the mass of cells moves slowly along the mother's fallopian tube to the uterus, where it is implanted in the uterine lining. During the implantation process, the placenta is formed. The **placenta** is a structure that serves as a life-support system for the fetus, allowing oxygen and nutrients to pass into the fetus and waste products to pass out.

The embryonic stage. The **embryonic stage** begins after the cell mass is implanted in the uterus and lasts from two weeks through week eight. Most of the vital organs and body systems form at this time.

The fetal stage. The **fetal stage** is the third stage of prenatal development and covers the period from the end of week eight to birth. Cells continue to divide, body structures become functional, and the fetus becomes capable of movement. When a fetus is from 22 to 26 weeks old, it may survive if birth occurs, but chances for survival increase the closer the term is to 36 weeks.

Prenatal risks. Risks during the prenatal period include the following.

- Adequate nutrition for the mother is imperative. Maternal **malnutrition** may affect not only the size of the infant but also the development of systems such as the immune system or the brain.

- **Teratogens** are agents or substances that can produce developmental malformations. Many environmental pollutants (some pesticides, for example), as well as drugs, both therapeutic and recreational (for example, alcohol, cocaine, marijuana, and nicotine), can damage a developing fetus. Drugs such as marijuana remain in the fat cells of the body for as long as 30 days, and other drugs can enter the semen. Consequently, if a father or mother takes drugs prior to conception or if a mother takes drugs at any time during gestation, the fetus may be seriously damaged. A mother's ingestion of alcohol during pregnancy can produce **fetal alcohol syndrome,** a complex of birth defects including retardation, lower birth weight, and distinct facial features—a flat nose, wide-set eyes, lack of an indentation on the upper lip (philtrum), and a thin upper lip. Ingestion of cocaine (or crack) during this period may produce a **cocaine-exposed infant,** one who is hyperactive, so sensitive to environmental stimulation that it can't tolerate being held, and possibly retarded. Tobacco use during pregnancy and passive ingestion of smoke from other smokers can also damage the fetus and increase the risk for miscarriage and birth complications as can use of amphetamines, barbiturates, and some tranquilizers.

Development in Infancy and Childhood

Physical development.

- In utero, the **brain** develops rapidly, and an infant is born with essentially all of the nerve cells it will ever have; brain development is particularly rapid during the third trimester. However, after birth, neural connections must form in order for the newborn ultimately to walk, talk, and remember. Mark Rosenzweig and David Krech conducted an experiment to demonstrate the importance of **enriched environments** during development. They compared rats raised alone to those that were allowed to use a playground in the company of other rats. Those in the impoverished (solitary) environment developed a thinner cortex with fewer **glial cells,** cells that support and nourish the brain's neurons. Other studies have demonstrated that stimulation provided by touch or massage benefits both premature babies and infant rats, a fact that argues for providing an enriched environment for a developing organism.

- Infants are born with a surprising number of unlearned (innate) **reflexes,** that is, unlearned responses to stimuli.

  —The **Moro reflex** is an outstretching of the arms and legs in response to a loud noise or sudden change in the environment. The infant's body tenses; arms are extended and then drawn inward as if embracing.

— The **Babinski reflex** is an outward projection of the big toe and fanning of the others when the sole of the foot is touched.

— The **sucking reflex** occurs when an object touches the lips.

— The **rooting reflex** is the turning of an infant's head toward a stimulus such as a breast or hand.

— The **grasping reflex** is the vigorous grasping of an object that touches the palm.

— The **plantar reflex** is the curling under of the toes when the ball of the foot is touched. Physicians sometimes use these reflexes to assess the rate of development. Gradually, learned responses replace the reflex actions as an infant becomes more responsive to the environment.

■ Although the rate of **motor development** can vary, the developmental sequence is the same. On average, an infant will learn to roll over at 2½ months, sit without support at 6 months, and walk alone at 12 months. The growth and body development from infant to child occurs in a **cephalocaudal direction;** that is, the head and upper trunk develop before the lower trunk and feet.

Sensory and perceptual development. Newborn infants can and do respond to a wide range of environmental stimuli. All human senses function to some degree at birth; touch is the most highly developed and vision is the least developed sense. At the age of 3 months, however, most infants can recognize a photograph of their mother. An infant's ability to perceive depth has been studied extensively with an apparatus called a **visual cliff,** a box with a glass platform that extends over a drop of several feet. An adult (mother or experimenter) stands on one side of the glass bridge and calls to the child, who is on the other. Eleanor Gibson and Richard Walk, in a well-known study, found that at about 6 months babies balk at crawling over the edge of the "cliff." Such a response indicates that depth perception is present at this age.

Cognitive development. The term **cognitive development** refers to the development of the ability to think and to mentally represent events and to manipulate symbols.

Jean Piaget, a pioneer in the study of children's thinking, was concerned with the way a child organizes information from the environment and adapts to it. He believed that every behavioral act requires two dynamic processes of adaptation: assimilation and accommodation. **Assimilation** is the process of acquiring new information about the world and fitting it to already acquired information. A child who calls all grown males "daddy," based on the child's perception that they and "daddy" are in some way similar, is practicing assimilation. **Accommodation** is the process of creating a new concept to handle new information; for example, children come to realize that all toys don't belong to them, that some belong to other children.

Piaget, who had a strong biological background, proposed four stages of development: sensorimotor, preoperational, concrete operational, and formal operational. According to Piaget,

- During the **sensorimotor stage** (birth to age 2) infants develop their ability to coordinate motor actions with sensory activity. At the start of this stage, children's behavior is dominated by reflexes, but by the end of it, they can use mental images. Also during this stage, children acquire the concept of **object permanence,** realizing that objects still exist even when the objects are not present.

- During the **preoperational stage** (ages 2 to 7 years), children improve in the use of mental images and symbolic thought. Most of the thinking of children of this age, however, is **egocentric** (self-centered).

- During the **concrete operational stage** (ages 7 to 11 years), children begin to develop many concepts and to organize the concepts into classes and categories.

- During the **formal operational stage** (ages 11 years and beyond), children learn to use and to manipulate abstract symbolic concepts, develop and mentally test hypotheses, and work mental problems. That is, they can reason.

Although Piaget's theories are subject to some criticism, they are widely used and important in guiding research in childhood cognitive development.

Language development. **Language acquisition** is one of the most important aspects of a child's development. Ages for types of acquisition vary, but the usual chronological course is as given in Table 7, page 183, in the chapter "Cognition and Language."

Moral development. Lawrence Kohlberg proposed that **moral development** occurs in three levels, with two stages at each level.

- **The preconventional level:**

  —At **stage 1, punishment orientation,** judgments are guided by the prospect of punishment.

  —At **stage 2, pleasure-seeking orientation,** activities are undertaken primarily to satisfy one's own needs; needs of others are important only as they relate to one's own needs.

- **The conventional level:**

  —At **stage 3, good girl/good boy orientation,** behavior is engaged in that brings approval or pleases others in a child's immediate group.

  —At **stage 4, authority orientation,** behavior is influenced by respect for authority, performing one's duty, and doing what is right.

- **The postconventional level:**

   —At **stage 5, contract and legal orientation,** behavior is based on support of rules and regulations because society's right to exact such support is accepted.

   —At **stage 6, ethical and moral principles orientation,** behavior is directed by self-chosen ethical and moral principles.

Kohlberg found that the first two stages are reached by most children, that stages 3 and 4 are reached by older children and most adults, but that the stage 6 is reached by only 20% of the population.

Carol Gilligan examined certain differences between the moral development of males and that of females. In younger children, she found that girls are more concerned with a morality based on caring and boys with a morality based on justice. Gilligan proposed that this **gender difference** is in part due to children's relationship with their mother.

Social development. **Social development** begins at birth as a child forms an **attachment** (a strong emotional bond) with the primary caregiver(s), usually the mother. Harry Harlow studied **attachment deprivation** with baby monkeys raised in isolation. Although their physical needs were met and they were given surrogate mothers made of cloth, these monkeys suffered severe behavior pathologies. They recovered if the isolation was limited to three months, but longer periods produced abnormal adults. Ethically, this type of study could not be conducted with humans, but parallels have been found with children reared in cold, isolated, emotionally deprived environments. Emotional attachments to caregivers are thought to be essential for social development.

Konrad Lorenz studied **imprinting,** a rapid and relatively permanent type of learning that occurs for a limited time (called a **critical period**) early in life, particularly in birds. Baby ducks learn to follow their mother if they see her moving during the first 30-hour period after their birth. If, however, they don't see their mother, they can imprint on and follow a human or even a moving object instead. Imprinting demonstrates that attachments by the young to a parent can occur early and can have lifelong consequences.

The term **gender stereotyping** refers to patterns of behavior expected of people according to their gender. The development of gender-related differences is complex. Gender stereotyping occurs not only because of parental differences in rearing children of each gender but also because of socialization experiences. Eleanor Maccoby has observed that children with widely different personalities play together simply because they are of the same gender.

Personality development. Developmental psychologists also study personality development in children. See page 114 for a discussion of Freud's and of Erikson's stages of personality development.

Development in Adolescence

Adolescence is the transition period from childhood to adulthood, a period that brings sometimes tumultuous physical, social, and emotional changes. Adolescence begins with the onset of **puberty** and extends to adulthood, usually spanning the years between 12 and 20. **Puberty** is the period during which the reproductive system matures, a process characterized by a marked increase in sex hormones.

Physical development. Physical development in adolescence includes a growth spurt as the body fills out, voice changes (especially in males), and an increase in sex hormones. Secondary sex characteristics, such as breasts in females and beards in males, appear. Girls' first menstruation (**menarche**) usually occurs between the ages of 11 and 14.

Social development. According to Erik Erikson, appropriate social development in adolescence requires solving the major challenge of **ego-identity vs. role diffusion.** (See Table 5, p. 115.) To resolve this life crisis, adolescents must form an ego-identity, a strong sense of "who I am and what I stand for," or they may suffer role diffusion (running from activity to activity), with the increased likelihood of succumbing to peer pressure.

Gender.

- **Gender differences** in behaviors or mental processes continue to develop during adolescence. Research has indicated that experience and learning have a greater impact on such behaviors than do biological factors.

- **Gender identity,** the recognition of being male or female, develops by age 3. Once they have established gender identity, children usually try to adapt their behavior and thoughts to accepted gender-specific roles.

- A **gender role** consists of the behaviors associated with one's gender. Gender-related activities help an individual to establish an identity. Sometimes a person adopts **gender-role stereotypes,** beliefs about the "typical" behavior of males and females expected by society.

- One meaning of the term **androgynous** is having adopted both behaviors associated with males and those associated with females. Androgynous males can do hard physical labor and yet care for babies; androgynous females can be homemakers and yet fix cars or drive taxis.

Peer pressure. **Peer pressure,** a term used to denote legitimization of activities by a peer group, has been used to explain many adolescent societal difficulties. Although a peer group rarely forces an adolescent to try new activities, it may legitimize those activities by indulging in them.

Sexual behavior. During the past few decades, the **sexual behavior** of adolescents has been heavily investigated. While the threat of AIDS (acquired immune deficiency syndrome) has changed some behaviors, many surveys indicate a dramatic increase in adolescent sexual activity through the twentieth century. The famous Kinsey survey in the 1940s reported that 50% of the men and 20% of the women surveyed reported having engaged in premarital intercourse by age 20. Three surveys in the 1980s found a substantial increase in the activity, with premarital intercourse reported by 68% of college men and 59% percent of college women. Studies have also shown that teenagers are still largely uninformed about contraception.

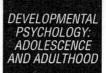

Problems during adolescence. Adolescent problems are many and often involve the adolescents' relationships with their peer group as well as their search for identity. These problems not only may affect physical survival in adolescents but also may have lifelong physical and psychological effects.

- **Substance abuse** is a major health threat. Legal and illegal substances available to adolescents include tobacco, caffeine, alcohol, glue, paint vapors, and pills. In one survey, 30% of the adolescents reported using illicit drugs, such as amphetamine and cocaine. The spread of AIDS infections by use of dirty needles increases the seriousness of this health threat.

- **Eating disorders** have increased dramatically among adolescents, particularly females. **Anorexia nervosa** is a voluntary weight loss of at least 25% of body weight; the extreme thinness may lead to other health problems such as cessation of menstruation. **Bulimia** is an eating disorder characterized by binges, purges with laxatives, and self-induced vomiting. Some people have alternating patterns of the two problems. A prolonged period of either eating disorder can result in serious health problems.

- **Suicides** and **attempted suicides** have increased among adolescents at alarming rates in recent decades. Research findings suggest that the suicidal adolescent has usually had, since childhood, a history of stress and personal problems. Attempts to resolve the problems, including running away from home and increasing social isolation, may precipitate an attempted suicide. Early professional help is often needed to prevent withdrawal and acting out of problems.

Personality Development

Two widely cited approaches to **personality development** are those of Sigmund Freud (also see p. 121) and Erik Erikson.

Sigmund Freud's stages of psychosexual development. Sigmund Freud developed a treatment theory called psychoanalysis, which is based upon a theory of **psychosexual stages** of development (Table 4).

FREUDIAN PSYCHOSEXUAL STAGES OF DEVELOPMENT		
Stage	**Age**	**Erogenous Zone / Activities**
Oral	0 to 18 months	Mouth / sucking, biting, chewing
Anal	18 to 36 months	Anus / bowel and bladder control
Phallic	3 to 6 years	Genitals / masturbation
Latency	6 years to puberty	— / repression of sexual feelings
Genital	puberty +	Maturation of sexual orientation

■ Table 4 ■

Erik Erikson's stages of development. Erik Erikson proposed a theory of development that continues throughout the life span. His theory states that there are universal **life stages** and that a specific **psychosocial dilemma** occurs at each phase of development. These problems (crises) must be resolved before an individual can move to the next developmental stage (Table 5). Erikson's theory has been credited for accounting for continuity and changes in personality development. It has also been criticized for vagueness and has not stimulated a great deal of empirical research.

ERIK ERIKSON'S STAGES OF DEVELOPMENT		
Age	**Psychological Stage**	**Period**
Birth to 1 year	*Trust vs. Mistrust* Learning that the provider of comfort is reliable, consistent, and predictable	Oral-sensory
2 to 3 years	*Autonomy vs. Shame and Doubt* Learning to exercise independence and freedom of choice along with self-control	Muscular-anal
3 to 5 years	*Initiative vs. Guilt* Planning and executing a task for the sake of actively doing it	Locomotor-genital
6 to 11 years	*Industry vs. Inferiority* Developing as a worker and producer	Latency
Adolescence	*Identity vs. Role Confusion* Evolving a sense of self that is reliable and consistent, both for oneself and for others	Puberty
Young adulthood	*Intimacy vs. Isolation* Preparing for a commitment to affiliation with others and developing the ethical strength to abide by such commitments	Young adulthood
Middle age	*Generativity vs. Stagnation* Finding a way to support in the establishment and guidance of the next generation	Adulthood
Old age	*Integrity vs. Despair* Integrating the earlier stages into an acceptance of oneself and a sense of fulfillment rather than looking back in regret at what might have been	Maturity

■ Table 5 ■

Development in Early and Middle Adulthood

Adulthood has no signpost to announce its onset (as adolescence is announced by puberty). In technologically advanced nations, the life span is more than 70 years. Developmental psychologists usually consider early adulthood to cover approximately age 20 to age 40 and middle adulthood approximately 40 to 65.

Early adulthood. In **early adulthood,** an individual is concerned with developing the ability to share intimacy, seeking to form relationships and find intimate love. Long-term relationships are formed, and often marriage and children result. The young adult is also faced with career decisions.

- Choices concerning **marriage** and **family** are often made during this period. Research shows that divorce is more likely among people who marry during adolescence, those whose parents were divorced, and those who are dissimilar in age, intelligence, personality, or attractiveness. Separation is also more frequent among those who do not have children. Most people who have divorced remarry; consequently, children may experience more than one set of parents.

- Such alternatives to marriage as "living together" (**cohabitation**) have become more common. In 1997, the Census Bureau estimated that 4.13 million unwed couples lived in the United States.

- **Work/career choice** affects not only socioeconomic status but also friends, political values, residence location, child care, job stress, and many other aspects of life. And while income is important in both career selection and career longevity, so are achievement, recognition, satisfaction, security, and challenge. In the modern cultures of many nations, the careers of both spouses or partners frequently must be considered in making job choices.

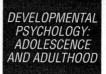
Middle adulthood. In **middle adulthood,** an important challenge is to develop a genuine concern for the welfare of future generations and to contribute to the world through family and work. Erik Erikson refers to the problem posed at this stage as **generativity vs. self-absorption** (Table 5, p. 115).

Robert Havighurst lists seven **major tasks** in the middle years.

- accepting and adjusting to physiological changes, such as menopause

- reaching and maintaining satisfaction in one's occupation

- adjusting to and possibly caring for aging parents

- helping teenage children to become responsible adults

- achieving adult social and civic responsibility

- relating to one's spouse as a person

- developing leisure-time activities

While a **midlife crisis** is not regarded as a universal phenomenon, during one's 40s and 50s comes the recognition that more than half of one's life is gone. That recognition may prompt some to feel that the clock is ticking and that they must make sudden, drastic changes in order to achieve their goals, while others focus on finding satisfaction with the present course of their lives.

Development in Late Adulthood

Late adulthood (old age) is generally considered to begin at about age 65. Erik Erikson suggests that at this time it is important to find meaning and satisfaction in life rather than to become bitter and disillusioned, that is, to resolve the conflict of **integrity vs. despair** (Table 5, p. 115). It has been estimated that by the year 2030, Americans over 65 will make up 20% of the population. Despite the problems associated with longevity, studies of people in their 70s have shown that growing old is not necessarily synonymous with substantial mental or physical deterioration. Many older people are happy and engaged in a variety of activities. **Gerontology,** an interdisciplinary field that studies the process of aging and the aging population, involves psychology, biology, sociology, and other fields.

Theories of successful aging. Theories of successful aging include the following:

- The **disengagement theory** states that as people age, their withdrawal from society is normal and desirable as it relieves them of responsibilities and roles that have become difficult. This process also opens up opportunities for younger people; society benefits as more-energetic young people fill the vacated positions.

- The **activity theory** contends that activity is necessary to maintain a "life of quality," that is, that one must "use it or lose it" no matter what one's age and that people who remain active in all respects—physically, mentally, and socially—adjust better to the aging process. Proponents of this theory believe that activities of earlier years should be maintained as long as possible.

Ageism. Ageism may be defined as the prejudice or discrimination that occurs on the basis of age. Although it can be used against people of all ages, older people are most frequently its target and it may often result in forced retirement. Stereotyping of the elderly is also an aspect of ageism, as seen in such a statement as "He drives like a little old lady."

Physical changes. People typically reach the peak of their physical strength and endurance during their twenties and then gradually decline. In later adulthood, a variety of physiological changes may occur, including some degree of atrophy of the brain and a decrease in the rate of neural processes. The respiratory and circulatory systems are less efficient, and changes in the gastrointestinal tract may lead to in-

creased constipation. Bone mass diminishes, especially among women, leading to bone density disorders such as osteoporosis. Muscles become weaker unless exercise programs are followed. The skin dries and becomes less flexible. Hair loss occurs in both sexes. There is also decreased sensitivity in all of the sensory modalities, including olfaction, taste, touch, hearing, and vision.

Cognitive changes. The study of cognitive changes in the older population is complex. Response speeds (neural and motor) have been reported to decline; some researchers believe that age-related decrease in working memory is the crucial factor underlying poorer performance by the elderly on cognitive tasks.

- **Intellectual changes** in late adulthood do not always result in reduction of ability. While **fluid intelligence** (the ability to see and to use patterns and relationships to solve problems) does decline in later years, **crystallized intelligence** (the ability to use accumulated information to solve problems and make decisions) has been shown to rise slightly over the entire life span. K. Warner Schaie and Sherry Willis reported that a decline in cognitive performance could be reversed in 40% to 60% of elderly people who were given remedial training.

- **Dementias** are usually responsible for cognitive defects seen in older people. These disorders, however, occur only in about 15% of people over 65. The leading cause of dementia in the United States is **Alzheimer's disease,** a progressive, eventually fatal disease that begins with confusion and memory lapses and ends with the loss of ability to care for oneself.

Retirement. Retirement at age 65 is the conventional choice for many people, although some work until much later. People have been found to be happier in retirement if they are not forced to retire before they are ready and if they have enough income to maintain an adequate living standard. Chronic health problems such as arthritis, rheumatism, and hypertension increasingly interfere with the quality of life of most individuals as they age.

Widowhood. Women tend to marry men older than they are and, on average, live 5 to 7 years longer than men. One study found ten times as many widows as widowers. Widowhood is particularly stressful if the death of the spouse occurs early in life; close support of friends, particularly other widows, can be very helpful.

Death and dying. Death and dying has been studied extensively by Elisabeth Kübler-Ross, who suggested that terminally ill patients display the following five basic reactions.

- **Denial,** an attempt to deny the reality and to isolate oneself from the event, is frequently the first reaction.
- **Anger** frequently follows, as the person envies the living and asks, "Why should I be the one to die?"
- **Bargaining** may occur; the person pleads to God or others for more time.
- As the end nears, recognition that death is inevitable and that separation from family will occur leads to feelings of exhaustion, futility, and deep **depression.**
- **Acceptance** often follows if death is not sudden, and the person finds peace with the inevitable.

People who are dying are sometimes placed in a **hospice,** a hospital for the terminally ill that attempts to maintain a good quality of life for the patient and the family during the final days. In a predictable pattern after a loved one's death, initial shock is followed by grief, followed by apathy and depression, which may continue for weeks. Support groups and counseling can help in successfully working through this process.

Personality can be defined as an individual's characteristic pattern of feeling, thinking, and acting. Theorists view personality from several diverse perspectives.

Psychodynamic Perspectives

Psychodynamic theories, descended from the work of Sigmund Freud, emphasize the importance of *unconscious* mental forces.

Freud and psychoanalytic theory. Sigmund Freud originated the **psychoanalytic** approach based on his experiences in his psychiatric practice and developed a technique called **free association,** which requires a patient to relax and report everything that comes to mind no matter how trivial or how strange it might seem. Using this technique, he found that patients often revived painful memories reaching back even to early childhood.

Freud believed that the mind is like an iceberg, mostly hidden (Figure 19), and that free association would ultimately let a patient retrieve memories from the unconscious, memories not ordinarily available because they are threatening in some way. **Conscious** awareness (the visible part of the iceberg) floats above the surface. The **preconscious** (the area only shallowly submerged) contains information which can voluntarily be brought to awareness. The **unconscious** (the larger, deeply submerged

Levels of Consciousness

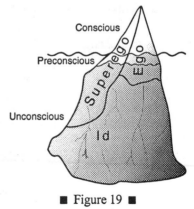

■ Figure 19 ■

portion of the iceberg) contains thoughts, feelings, and memories of which a person is unaware and many of which have been **repressed,** or forcibly blocked from consciousness. From his work, Freud developed **psychoanalysis,** a technique for treating psychological disorders by identifying and resolving problems stored in the unconscious.

Freudian personality theory. Concomitant with his development of psychoanalysis, Freud constructed a theory of personality, which includes the following observations.

- Personality has three **structures:** the id, the ego, and the superego. The **id,** a reservoir of unconscious psychic energy, operates on the **pleasure principle,** seeks immediate gratification, and is not restrained by reality. It operates solely at the unconscious level. The **ego,** which develops in early childhood, operates through the **reality principle,** which seeks to gratify impulses of the id realistically and to bring long-term pleasure without pain. The ego operates at both the conscious and preconscious levels. The **superego,** a third structure, emerges as children reach 4 or 5 and internalize the morals of parents and society. The superego acts as a voice of conscience and operates mostly at the preconscious level of awareness. People also possess and are driven by a psychological energy called the **libido.**

- Children pass through a series of **psychosexual stages** during which the id seeks pleasure from body areas, **erogenous zones,** that change during development (Table 4, p. 114). If children have difficulty passing through a particular stage, they are said to have become **fixated.** Fixation at the **phallic stage** may create an **Oedipus complex** for a boy (jealousy of a son toward his father in competing for his mother's attention) or an **Electra complex** for a girl (who competes with her mother for her father's attention). Children resolve these conflicts by **identifying** with the parent of the same gender.

- During a child's development, the ego strategically uses **defense mechanisms** to deal with the **anxiety** produced by conflicting impulses from the id (operating on the pleasure principle) and the superego (using internalized representation of the parents' value system). Defense mechanisms include

  — **repression,** preventing dangerous or painful thoughts from entering consciousness

  — **reaction formation,** preventing expression of dangerous impulses by exaggerating opposite behavior

  — **projection,** attributing one's feelings, shortcomings, or unacceptable impulses to others

  — **displacement,** directing impulses toward a less threatening or more acceptable person or object

  — **regression,** retreating to an earlier stage of development

  — **sublimation,** rechanneling of unacceptable impulses into acceptable activities

  — **denial,** refusing to perceive reality, acting as if something did not happen

  — **compensation,** counteracting real or imagined difficulties or weaknesses by emphasizing other traits or excelling in other areas

  — **intellectualization,** separating emotions from threatening situations by thinking and acting impersonally

  — **fantasy,** meeting unfulfilled desires by imagination

- **Psychopathology** can result if an individual does not pass through the stages of psychosexual development and becomes fixated, or fails to pass to the next stage. For example, a person fixated at the oral stage could, among other things, exhibit symptoms of obsessive eating or smoking in adult life. The problem could be identified and treated through psychoanalysis.

The neo-Freudians. Other theorists, while they accepted much of the Freudian theory, differed on certain basic premises and introduced additional ideas.

- **Carl Jung,** a contemporary of Freud, developed a variation of psychoanalytic theory called **analytical psychology,** which includes two well-known concepts.

  —The **collective unconscious,** in contrast with Freud's **unconscious,** contains latent memory traces from a person's ancestors.

  —**Archetypes,** emotionally charged images and thoughts that have universal meaning, may be manifested in a culture's symbols, art, religion, and so forth.

- **Alfred Adler**'s approach to personality theory is called **individual psychology,** which de-emphasizes the importance of sexual motivation and focuses on socially based motives. Adler believed that the behavior of adults is motivated by **striving for superiority,** a drive for perfection.

- **Karen Horney** proposed that many adult characteristics are produced by attempts to deal with **basic anxiety,** a feeling of being isolated and helpless in a potentially hostile world. Horney was also a pioneer in the study of psychology of women. She suggested that outside the family, women experience harmful effects because society places a greater value on being male, an attitude that contributes to women's feeling of inferiority and lack of self-esteem.

Trait and Type Perspectives

A **trait** is a characteristic pattern of behavior or conscious motive which can be self-assessed or assessed by peers. The term **type** is used to identify a certain collection of traits that make up a broad, general personality classification.

Trait theories.

- **Gordon Allport** proposed that an individual's conscious motives and traits better describe personality than does that person's unconscious motivation. He identified three types of traits:

    — **Cardinal traits,** such as a tendency to seek out the truth, govern the direction of one's life.

    — **Central traits** operate in daily interactions, as illustrated by a tendency to always try to control a situation.

    — **Secondary traits,** such as a tendency to discriminate against older people, involve response to a specific situation,

- **Raymond Cattell,** by means of a statistical technique called **factor analysis,** organized the huge number of words used generally to describe personality (over 17,000) and reduced them to 16 basic factors.

    — emotional, easily upset vs. calm, stable

    — intelligent vs. unintelligent

    — suspicious vs. trusting

    — reserved, unfriendly vs. outgoing, friendly

    — assertive, dominant vs. not assertive, humble

    — sober, serious vs. happy-go-lucky

    — conscientious vs. expedient

    — shy, timid vs. venturesome

    — tender-minded vs. tough-minded

    — practical vs. imaginative

    — shrewd vs. forthright

    — self-assured, placid vs. apprehensive

    — conservative vs. experimenting

    — group oriented vs. self-sufficient

    — undisciplined vs. self-disciplined

    — relaxed vs. tense, driven

Type theories.

■ **Hans Eysenck** proposed a higher organization of personality traits into three basic groups (traits plus their opposites), which, he suggested, constituted **types.**

— extraversion (as opposed to introversion)

— neuroticism (as opposed to emotional stability)

— psychoticism (as opposed to impulse control)

■ **The Big Five.** In recent years, theorists have felt the need for more personality dimensions than Eysenck's three. The five independent dimensions, selected using statistical procedures, are known as the **"Big Five."**

— extraversion/introversion: characteristics described in terms such as talkative, sociable, adventurous vs. reticent, turned inward

— agreeableness/antagonism: characteristics described in terms such as good-natured, cooperative, likable vs. hostile, spiteful

— conscientiousness/undirectedness: characteristics described in terms such as responsible, neat, task motivated vs. disorganized

— stability/instability: characteristics described in terms such as calm, poised, composed vs. uncertain, insecure

— openness to experience/conforming: characteristics described in terms such as flexible, original, independent, creative, daring vs. rigid, conventional, conforming, noncreative, timid

The Humanistic Perspective

The **humanistic perspective** focuses on the positive image of what it means to be human. Human nature is viewed as basically good, and humanistic theorists focus on methods that allow fulfillment of potential.

- **Abraham Maslow** proposed that an individual is motivated by a **hierarchy of needs.** Basic needs must be met before higher ones can be satisfied. Arranged in order from lowest to highest (in a *hierarchy*), the needs are

  —physiological (satisfaction of hunger and thirst)

  —safety (security)

  —belongingness and love (being loved, avoiding loneliness)

  —esteem (achievement, recognition, self-esteem)

  —self-actualization (realization of one's full potential).

  Maslow also believed that the achievement of self-actualization is often marked by peak experiences, feelings of incredible peace and happiness in the course of life activities.

- **Carl Rogers,** a clinical psychologist, used the theory of **self-concept,** which he defined as an organized pattern of perceived characteristics along with the values attached to those attributes. He also assumed that within each individual there is a biological drive toward growth of self-concept, which can ultimately lead to **self-actualization.** Rogers believed that while children's self-concept is developing, they may internalize **conditions of worth,** judgments about the kinds of behaviors that will bring approval from others. He felt that, to promote growth and development, parents and authority figures should give a child unconditional acceptance and love, which allows a child to develop self-acceptance and to achieve self-actualization. To help his clients get back on the road to self-actualization, he developed a therapeutic approach called **client-centered therapy,** in which the therapist offers the client **unconditional positive regard** by supporting the client regardless of what is said. The warm, sympathetic therapeutic environment allows the client to be freed of internalized conditions of worth and to resume the self-actualization process.

Behavioral Approaches

Although **behavioral personality theory** involves the study of personality through behaviorism (which emphasizes overt, objective behavior), theorists in this area also consider cognitive processes and study particular ways of learning, such as by observing others in a social context. Traditional learning procedures—classical conditioning, operant conditioning (instrumental learning), and observational learning, p. 60—are used to demonstrate how people learn many emotional responses.

- **John Dollard** and **Neal Miller** suggested, based on basic principles of learning theory, that habits that are reinforced tend to be repeated and eventually become part of a stable array of habits that form personality.

- **Alfred Bandura** believed that much of our learning, and consequently many aspects of behavior and personality, takes place through observing the behavior of others and using **observational behavior** for **modeling** (p. 68). According to Bandura, learning involves not only connections between stimuli and responses but also **cognitive representation** and **rearrangement.** A child, for example, who sees that cheating leads to punishment and honesty to rewards (cognitive representation) decides to model honest behavior (rearrangement). He used the term **self-efficacy** to describe a person's belief in his or her capability of successfully executing a specific behavior. A strong sense of self-efficacy allows a person to feel free to select, try, and complete behaviors leading to desired outcomes. Self-efficacy is based upon feelings of **self-worth;** people with high levels of self-efficacy are more likely to attribute success to themselves rather than to chance or to others and to continue to select and control circumstances of their lives.

Personality Assessment

Personality assessment is conducted through behavioral observations, paper-and-pencil tests, and projective techniques. To be useful, such assessments must be constructed using the established criteria of standardization, reliability, and validity. (See p. 165 for a discussion of test construction.) The information can be used in several areas, including clinical work, vocational counseling, education, and research.

Behavioral observations. Most people use **behavioral observations** to form impressions of others. Such observations are also an important part of clinical assessments by clinical psychologists and other professionals.

Interviews, during which subjects' behaviors are observed, may be structured or unstructured. The examiner may ask a standardized set of questions (**structured interview**) or engage in a conversational interchange with the subject (**unstructured interview**). During the interview, the examiner forms an opinion about personality characteristics (as is done, for example, also in the nonclinical setting of a job interview).

Paper-and-pencil tests. The many and various **paper-and-pencil tests** are used for a variety of purposes. To be useful, such tests must be **reliable** (that is, they must yield very close scores each time they are administered to a particular individual) and **valid** (that is, they must measure what they are designed to measure). The **Minnesota Multiphasic Personality Inventory** (**MMPI**) (*multiphasic,* many phased, because the test simultaneously measures a number of personality dimensions) is widely used to identify personality problems. The **California Personality Inventory** (**CPI**) is also used extensively, generally with people who do not have personality problems. Some tests assess personality as defined by a particular theory. For example, **Cattell's 16 PF** (personality factor) questionnaire assesses the personality traits defined in Cattell's trait theory.

Projective techniques. **Projective techniques** assess personality by presenting ambiguous stimuli and requiring a subject to respond, *projecting* his or her personality into the responses.

- The ambiguous inkblots in the well-known **Rorschach inkblot test,** developed by Hermann Rorschach, are perceived differently by different people, and those perceptions are believed to be related to the subjects' problems.

- The **Thematic Apperception Test (TAT),** developed by Henry Murray, consists of a series of ambiguous pictures, which the subject is requested to describe and tell a story about. The test is used to identify a person's emotions, motives, and problems.

Scoring and interpreting projective tests requires special training, but the tests can be very helpful in identifying personality problems.

Those in the field of **abnormal psychology** study people's emotional, cognitive, and/or behavioral problems. **Abnormal behavior** may be defined as behavior that is disturbing (socially unacceptable), distressing, maladaptive (or self-defeating), and often the result of distorted thoughts (cognitions).

Perspectives on Abnormal Behavior

Several perspectives (models, approaches derived from data) and theories attempt to explain the causes of abnormal behavior.

The medical perspective. Those who hold a **medical perspective** focus on biological and physiological factors as causes of abnormal behavior, which is treated as a disease, or **mental illness,** and is diagnosed through symptoms and cured through treatment. Hospitalization and drugs are often preferred methods of treatment rather than psychological investigation. (Recent research linking biochemical disorders with some abnormal behaviors has provided some support for this approach.)

The psychodynamic perspective. The **psychodynamic perspective,** proposed as an alternative to the medical model, evolved from Freudian psychoanalytic theory, which contends that psychological disorders are the consequence of anxiety produced by unresolved, unconscious conflicts. Treatment focuses on identification and resolution of the conflicts.

The behavioral perspective. Those espousing a **behavioral perspective** contend that abnormal behavior results from faulty or ineffective learning and conditioning. Treatments are designed to reshape disordered behavior and, using traditional learning procedures, to teach new, more appropriate, and more adaptive responses. For example, a behavioral analysis of a case of child abuse might suggest that a father abuses his children because he learned the abusive behavior from his father and must now learn more appropriate parenting tactics.

The cognitive perspective. According to the **cognitive perspective,** people engage in abnormal behavior because of particular thoughts and behaviors that are often based upon their false assumptions. Treatments are oriented toward helping the maladjusted individual develop new thought processes and new values. Therapy is a process of unlearning maladaptive habits and replacing them with more useful ones.

The social-cultural perspective. From the **social-cultural perspective,** abnormal behavior is learned within a social context ranging from the family, to the community, to the culture. Cultural variables, acquired through learning and cognitive processes, are believed to be important in producing abnormal behavior. Anorexia nervosa and bulimia, for example, are psychological disorders found mostly in Western cultures, which value the thin female body.

Diagnosis of Psychological Disorders

The diagnosis of a psychological disorder requires evaluation by a trained mental-health professional and usually an interview, administration of a variety of personality tests (and in some cases, neuropsychological tests), and gathering of background (including medical) information about the individual. The mental-health professional arrives at a diagnosis by comparing this information to that in the *Diagnostic and Statistical Manual of Mental Disorders,* the **DSM-IV** (IV for fourth edition, 1994), which uses a system devised by the

American Psychiatric Association to classify psychological disorders. The classification system, which lists 16 categories of maladjustment and more than 200 subcategories, is designed to improve the reliability of diagnoses by using observable behaviors to categorize disorders and to ensure that diagnoses are consistent with current information. Diagnosis using this resource requires the use of five dimensions, or **axes.** Judgments must be made on each of the five axes, and a diagnostician must consider a broad range of information in making the diagnosis.

The classification of abnormal behavior is made on the basis of **Axis I (Clinical Syndromes)** and **Axis II (Personality Disorders).** Patients may receive a diagnosis on both axes; the milder, long-standing personality disorders of Axis II may coexist with Axis I syndromes. The remaining three axes—**Axis III (General Medical Conditions), Axis IV (Psychosocial and Environmental Problems),** and **Axis V (Global Assessment of Functioning)**—are used to provide supplementary information. Use of the combined axes, which include the individual's history and highest level of competent functioning in the past year, ensures that a person not only will be assigned to a mental-disturbance category but also will be characterized by a number of relevant clinical factors.

Use of a classification system permits mental-health professionals to communicate accurately, helps in the determination of effective treatments, facilitates the use of research data on a particular category, and assists in making predictions. Classification systems, however, are based upon judgments of professionals and can change over time as new information is collected. Controversy still exists over the DSM-IV system; it is revised as new research information becomes available. Diagnostic categories have been deleted or changed. For example, "homosexuality" has been excluded as a mental-disturbance category, and arguments about use of the category "premenstrual syndrome" have resulted in the condition's being moved to the appendix, where it is called "premenstrual dysphoric disorder" and listed as needing more study. The category termed **"neuroses"** has not been included since the 1980 edition. The term **"psychosis"** is still used for conditions such as schizophrenia, which are characterized by bizarre behavior and beliefs, delusions, and loss of contact with reality.

Classification of Psychological Disorders

Classification of psychological disorders requires that symptoms be identified; sets of symptoms form a **syndrome.** Several of the most prevalent of the DSM-IV's 16 categories of disorders follow.

Anxiety disorders. Anxiety is a diffuse, extremely unpleasant feeling of vulnerability, apprehension, and fear. Symptoms of **anxiety disorders** include motor tension (trembling, jumpiness, inability to relax), hyperactivity (racing heart, dizziness, perspiration), and apprehension (disturbing thoughts). The following five (of the thirteen in the DSM-IV) types of anxiety disorders are well known.

- A **generalized anxiety disorder (GAD)** is a condition characterized by excessive anxiety and worrying, occurring more days than not for a period of at least six months. Anxiety is not triggered by any particular object or event but seems to be what Freud called **free-floating anxiety,** anxiety that is general and pervasive.

- A **phobic disorder** is marked by a continual, irrational fear of a specific situation or object such as snakes, heights, being closed in a small place, or leaving the home environment. Each **phobia** has a different name depending on the thing feared, such as **acrophobia,** a fear of high places; **agoraphobia,** a fear of open spaces; and **social phobia,** a fear of social or performance situations in which embarrassment may occur.

- A **panic disorder** is characterized by a chronic state of tension that can erupt in sudden episodes of intense panic or dread that last several minutes (or hours) and may include a variety of symptoms such as chest pains, trembling, and dizziness.

- An **obsessive-compulsive disorder** is an extreme preoccupation with certain thoughts and compulsive performance of particular behaviors. An **obsession** is the unsolicited reoccurrence of disturbing thoughts; a **compulsion** is a repetitive behavior (such as checking door locks) or mental activity (counting, praying, etc.) that one feels *compelled* to do, even against one's will. An example of the disorder is the compulsion to wash one's hands repeatedly, often to the extent of making them sore.

- **A post-traumatic stress disorder** is characterized by the reexperiencing of a traumatic event, symptoms of increased arousal, avoidance of reminders of the original trauma, and diminished interest in daily activities. Many war veterans retain vivid memories of (flashbacks) and nightmares about traumatic events experienced during battle.

While the causes of anxiety disorders are not completely understood, it is generally believed that some of the disorders (such as specific phobias, obsessive-compulsive disorders, and panic disorders) may have a genetic basis. One cause may be the inadequate action of the neurotransmitter **gamma-aminobutyric acid (GABA)**. Certain drugs, such as Valium and Librium, which increase the sensitivity of the GABA receptors, help reduce anxiety.

Somatoform disorders. A **somatoform disorder** is characterized by one or more symptoms of a physical dysfunction but for which there is no identifiable organic cause. Following are two examples (from seven in the DSM-IV).

- **A conversion disorder** is a condition manifested by a physical dysfunction (blindness, deafness, paralysis, numbness, etc.) that has no underlying organic basis. This condition (formerly called **hysteria**) allows escape from an anxiety-provoking activity. For example, an athlete who dreads competing in an event, might develop a numb arm and effectively avoid the event.

- **Hypochondriasis** is characterized by a continuing belief that one has one or more serious illnesses although no medical evidence supports the belief. An occasional headache, for example, may be interpreted by a hypochondriac as a brain tumor even though medical tests do not support this interpretation.

Dissociative disorders. In **dissociative disorders,** a part of an individual's personality becomes separate (dissociated) from other parts, producing a lack of integration of identity, memory, or consciousness. The DSM-IV lists five forms; the three most common follow.

- In **dissociative amnesia,** an individual develops a sudden inability to recall important personal information (such as her or his name); the disorder often follows psychological trauma. The memory loss cannot be attributed to physical trauma, a particular medical condition, or direct effects of drugs. Memory recall may occur suddenly or gradually.

- People experiencing a **dissociative fugue** suddenly and unexpectedly travel away from their home or customary place of activities and are unable to recall some or all of their past. They are confused about their personal identity, may not remember who they are, and sometimes assume a new identity. Recovery may be rapid.

- A **dissociative identity disorder** (formerly, multiple personality disorder) is characterized by the assuming of two or more distinct, integrated personalities, each of which manifests itself at times. The behaviors are accompanied by an inability, too extensive to be explained by ordinary forgetfulness, to recall important personal information. One personality may have no memory of the other(s). Often these disorders stem from childhood trauma such as sexual abuse.

Mood disorders. **Mood disorders** are characterized primarily by a disturbance in mood. (Remember, however, that all psychological disorders affect one's mood, or **affect.**) Two mood disorders (from four in the DSM-IV) are described below in more detail.

- In **major depressive disorder,** a person, for no apparent reason, experiences at least two or more weeks of depressed moods, feelings of worthlessness, and diminished interest or pleasure in most activities. To be classified as a major depressive disorder, the episode must be accompanied by clinically significant distress and impairment in social, occupational, or other areas of daily living.

- In a **bipolar disorder,** a person alternates between the hopelessness and lethargy of depression and the overexcited state of **mania.** Mania is manifested by hyperactivity and wild excitement. A person suffering from this disorder may lose control and act very inappropriately and sometimes destructively. (Subcategories of bipolar disorders are classified depending on the ratios of manic and depressive episodes.)

The causes of mood disorders have been the subject of much research. It is known that genetic factors are involved. (If one identical twin is diagnosed as having a major mood disorder, the chances are one in two that the other twin will also suffer such a disorder.) Biochemical factors also play a role. Norepinephrine, a neurotransmitter, is present in excessive amounts during mania and at low levels during depression. Serotonin, another neurotransmitter, is at low levels during depression. Drugs that regulate the level of these neurotransmitters (tricyclic antidepressants; monoamine oxidase, MAO, inhibitors; and selective serotonin-reuptake inhibitors, SSRIs) are used for treatment of the depressions. Research has also shown that cognitive factors, such as self-defeating reactions to events, contribute to the development of depression. An individual who accepts sole blame for all of life's happenings is more likely to develop depression. (Also see the discussion of treatments, p. 145.)

Schizophrenia and other psychotic disorders. Schizophrenic disorders are severe disorders characterized by distorted thoughts and perceptions, atypical communication, inappropriate emotion, abnormal motor behavior, and social withdrawal. The slow-developing schizophrenia known as **chronic** or **process schizophrenia** has a poor prognosis for recovery; when a formerly well-adjusted individual develops schizophrenia (known as **reactive** or **acute schizophrenia**), there is a better chance of recovery. The five major types of schizophrenia are as follows.

- **Paranoid schizophrenia** is characterized by prominent delusions or auditory hallucinations in the context of relative preservation of usual cognitive functioning and affect. (Examples are delusions of persecution, grandeur, or both.) Paranoid schizophrenics trust no one and are constantly on guard because they are convinced that others are plotting against them. They may seek retaliation against imagined enemies.

- **Catatonic schizophrenia** is evidenced by excessive, sometimes violent motor activity or by a mute, unresponsive, stuporous condition in which a person may retain the same posture for hours. A person may remain in one state for a long period or alternate between violent activity and remaining stiff and immobile, totally unresponsive to the outside world.

- **Disorganized (hebephrenic) schizophrenia** is characterized by bizarre symptoms, including extreme delusions, hallucinations, and inappropriate patterns of speech, mood, and movement. Inappropriate moods may be manifested by laughing or crying at unsuitable times.

- **Undifferentiated schizophrenia** is manifested by delusions, hallucinations, incoherent speech, and disorganized behavior. The conglomerate of symptoms fit the criteria of more than one type or of no clear type of schizophrenia.

- **Residual schizophrenia** is a condition in which at least one episode of schizophrenia has occurred although there are currently no prominent psychotic symptoms (for example, delusions or hallucinations). Certain negative symptoms, those indicating a lack, such as flat affect, poverty of speech, and avolition (lack of using the will, or choosing), continue, however, as do two or more attenuated positive symptoms (eccentric behavior, odd beliefs, and so forth). The course of this type of schizophrenia may be time limited and may represent a transitional phase between remission and a full-blown psychotic episode.

The causes of schizophrenia are complex and still not completely understood. It is known that genetic factors are involved because schizophrenia is found repeatedly in certain families; adult children of schizophrenic parents are more likely to develop schizophrenia than are children of nonschizophrenic parents. However, inheritance does not completely explain the etiology (cause) of schizophrenia (only 46% of identical twins of schizophrenic twins develop the disorder), and currently, a biochemical factor is also deemed important. Autopsies on some schizophrenics have found an excess of **dopamine** receptors, and drugs that block the activity of that neurotransmitter help control schizophrenic symptoms. In addition, misuse of amphetamines, which are similar to dopamine and which may increase the level of dopamine in the brain, produces many symptoms similar to those found in schizophrenia. In the brain structures of schizophrenics, other variations from the norm also occur, such as a smaller thalamus and enlarged ventricles. The complete etiology of schizophrenia remains a focus of research in psychopathology.

Personality disorders. **Personality disorders** are longstanding, maladaptive, and inflexible ways of relating to others, and the behaviors or symptoms characteristic of them usually begin in childhood or adolescence. Those with personality disorders may function adequately and be regarded simply as eccentric, but when they are faced with an extremely stressful situation, they can respond only rigidly and narrowly. The eleven types of personality disorders are classified in three groups, or clusters, based on their similarities. The disorders often emerge during childhood, adolescence, and early adulthood and continue into adult life.

- **Cluster A—disorders of odd/eccentric reactions**

    —A **paranoid** personality disorder is manifested by a pervasive distrust and suspiciousness of others and a tendency to interpret the actions of others as malevolent or threatening.

— A **schizoid** personality disorder is characterized by a tendency to be indifferent to social relationships and by restricted expression of emotions in interpersonal settings.

— Those with a **schizotypal** personality disorder display eccentric ways of thinking, perceiving, communicating, and behaving and are acutely uncomfortable in close relationships.

■ **Cluster B—disorders of dramatic, emotional, or erratic reactions**

— Individuals with an **antisocial** personality disorder manifest a pervasive tendency to disregard and to violate the rights of others.

— A **borderline** personality disorder is characterized by instability of interpersonal relationships, self-image, and emotions as well as by marked impulsivity.

— Those with a **histrionic** personality disorder exhibit pervasive and excessive emotionality and attention-seeking behavior.

— Manifestations of a **narcissistic** personality disorder include a pervasive pattern of grandiosity, a need for admiration, and a lack of empathy.

■ **Cluster C—disorders involving anxiety and fearfulness**

— Those with an **avoidant** personality disorder exhibit, in a variety of contexts, a pervasive pattern of social inhibition, feelings of inadequacy, and hypersensitivity to negative evaluations.

— Those with a **dependent** personality disorder allow others to make decisions and display a need to be taken care of that leads to submissive and clinging behavior accompanied by fears of separation.

— An **obsessive-compulsive** personality disorder involves, in many contexts, a tendency toward perfectionism, a rigid preoccupation with orderliness, and mental and interpersonal control at the expense of flexibility, openness, and efficiency.

- A disorder termed a **personality disorder not otherwise specified** is one that does not meet the criteria for a specific personality disorder but in which the combination of symptoms causes clinically significant distress or impairment in functioning.

Delirium, dementia, amnestic, and other cognitive disorders. Cognitive disorders involve a clinically significant deficit in cognition or memory that represents a marked change from a previous level of functioning. The disorders are usually further categorized based on their presumed etiology.

- A **delirium** is characterized by a disturbance in consciousness and a change in cognition that develop over a short time. Some examples are **delirium due to a medical condition,** and **substance-induced delirium** (such as caused by a drug of abuse or a toxin). Drugs that are listed as causing the condition include alcohol, amphetamines, caffeine, cocaine, hallucinogens, inhalants, marijuana, nicotine, opiates, phencyclidine (PCP), sedatives, and other unspecified chemicals. Substance withdrawal may also produce a delirium.

- A **dementia** is characterized by multiple cognitive deficits that include memory impairment. Examples are **dementia of Alzheimer's type, vascular dementia,** and **dementia due to HIV disease.**

- An **amnestic disorder** is shown by multiple cognitive deficits that include memory impairment, but the disorder is not connected with states of delerium or dementia. A major problem is the transfer of information from short term to long term memory. Amnestic disorders result from a physical cause such as a traumatic event (for example, a head injury incurred in an accident, during surgery, or from an electric shock), drug abuse, or the use of medications.

■ A fourth category, **cognitive disorder not otherwise specified,** is used to delineate a cognitive dysfunction presumed to be due to a general medical condition or substance use but that does not meet the other diagnostic criteria.

Eating disorders. **Eating disorders** are characterized by severe disturbances in eating behavior.

■ **Anorexia nervosa** is characterized by a refusal to maintain a minimally normal weight, intense fear of gaining weight, and distortion in the perception of the shape or size of one's body. Postmenarcheal females with this condition are often amenorrheic (having missed three consecutive menstrual cycles). Muscular weakness and osteoporosis (bone loss) may also occur.

■ **Bulimia nervosa** is manifested by binge eating and use of inappropriate techniques, such as purging or use of laxatives, to prevent weight gain. To qualify for this diagnosis, an individual must engage in binge eating and the inappropriate compensatory acts (purging, use of laxatives), on average, twice a week for three months.

Other disorders. DSM-IV diagnostic categories not described above include "substance-related disorders"; "disorders usually first diagnosed in infancy, childhood, or adolescence"; "sexual and gender identity disorders"; "sleep disorders"; "impulse-control disorders not elsewhere classified"; "adjustment disorders"; and "other conditions that may be a focus of clinical attention."

Legal Aspects of Psychological Disorders

Insanity is a legal concept. A person judged to have been insane at the time he or she committed a crime cannot be held responsible for those actions. **Competency,** also a legal concept, refers to defendants' capability of standing trial, that is, understanding a trial's purpose and procedures and cooperating in their own defense, at the time of trial. No simple relationships exist between diagnosed psychological disorders and court findings of insanity. If defendants are declared insane or incompetent, they are usually provided mental health treatment. The nature of the treatment depends upon a variety of factors including the mental disorder diagnosis.

A variety of treatments are available for those who experience difficulty in coping with their problems. There are two general categories of treatment: psychotherapy and biologically centered treatment. The over 200 types of **psychotherapy** use psychological techniques to treat emotional or behavioral problems and may deal with individuals or groups, children or adults. Therapists choose an approach (or approaches) consistent with their training and the problems and goal(s) of their clients. **Biomedical therapy** focuses on somatic (body) treatment and usually employs medications.

The Training of Psychotherapists

The training of psychotherapists varies widely. Examples of disciplines studied and degrees earned are given in Table 6.

TRAINING OF PSYCHOTHERAPISTS	
Discipline	**Degree**
Psychologist	PhD (Doctor of Philosophy) or PsyD (Doctor of Psychology)
Psychiatrist	MD (Doctor of Medicine)
Social worker	MSW (Master of Social Work)
Psychiatric nurse	BSN (Bachelor of Science in Nursing) or MA (Master of Arts)
Counselor	MA (Master of Arts in Counseling)

■ Table 6 ■

Psychotherapies

Psychodynamic therapies. Psychodynamic therapies, generally lengthy, "insight" therapies based on the psychoanalytic therapy developed by Freud, involve two major techniques. **Free association** requires clients to report anything that comes to mind. The intent of the process is to allow access to the **unconscious. Dream analysis** requires clients to report their dreams, which are then interpreted to provide insight into unconscious conflicts and motivations. A therapist uses these two processes to find commonalities in clients' thoughts and behaviors and to **interpret** them in terms of clients' problems.

At times, the treatment process is blocked by clients' **resistance** (unwillingness to provide information). **Transference** is a condition in which clients begin to consider their therapist in the same emotional light they would consider a person emotionally important in their lives, such as a parent or sibling. Dealing with interpretation, resistance, and transference is sometimes called **working through,** a therapeutic technique in which a therapist helps clients understand their conflicts and how to resolve them.

Humanistic therapies. Humanistic therapies deal with conscious (rather than unconscious) thoughts and with present (rather than past) occurrences and are conducted with goals of client growth and fulfillment.

Person-centered therapy. Carl Rogers developed **person-centered therapy** and advocated a warm, supportive environment (**unconditional positive regard**) in which a person feels completely accepted, can reveal true feelings, and can thus experience **self-growth** (an increase in self-esteem). Rogers suggested that people grow up in a world in which there are **conditions of worth** (that is, they learn that they will be rewarded only if they meet certain conditions and standards imposed by others), a situation that may result in low self-esteem. Rogers stressed the need for therapists to use **empathy,** identification with their clients.

Gestalt therapy. In Gestalt therapy, developed by Frederick "Fritz" Perls, therapists **challenge** clients with questions so that clients increase their awareness of feelings and develop the ability to face daily-living problems. Gestalt therapists also use a variety of other techniques, such as **role playing** and **confrontation,** to help clients learn to cope. Although Gestalt therapy directs clients more than does person-centered therapy, the therapies are similar in that both encourage clients to assume responsibility for the activities of life.

Existential therapy. **Existential therapy,** an "insight" therapy based on a client's developing insight, or self-understanding, focuses on problems of living such as choice, meaning, responsibility, and death. It emphasizes **free will,** the ability of humans to make choices that have not been dictated by heredity or past conditioning and through which a person can become the individual that she or he wants to be. The therapy attempts to restore meaning to life so that one has the courage to make choices that are both rewarding and socially constructive. After his experiences in a Nazi concentration camp, Victor Frankl developed a type of existential therapy called **logotherapy.** Frankl believed that prisoners who survived did so because they maintained **logos,** a sense of meaning. The therapy is directed toward helping clients reappraise what is really important (meaningful) in life.

Behavior therapies. **Behavior therapies** use learning principles to eliminate or to reduce maladaptive behavior(s). This therapeutic approach does not deal with unconscious conflicts but uses principles of social learning and personality theory to assist individuals in forming accurate perceptions of their feelings and of themselves. Behavior therapists focus on teaching clients to extinguish (unlearn) maladaptive behaviors (those based on groundless fears, for example), which they feel are acquired through classical and operant conditioning (p. 60) in day-to-day living. In turn, these same learning procedures can be used to extinguish maladaptive behaviors.

- **Systematic desensitization** (developed by Joseph Wolpe) requires clients to learn to associate deep relaxation with successive visualizations of anxiety-provoking stimuli or situations. Initially clients are taught to relax, next to visualize fearful items or events, and then to combine relaxation with the visualization. This procedure has been found to be especially effective in dealing with phobias.

- In **implosive therapy,** clients must imagine and deal with their worst fears in the safe surroundings of a therapist's office, a procedure which often leads to extinction of the anxiety.

- In **flooding,** clients, accompanied by a therapist, are placed in the real situation they dread in order to face and extinguish, their fear. For example, a person with **agoraphobia** (fear of open places) might be accompanied by a therapist into a store or crowd.

- **Biofeedback** requires that a bodily function (such as heart rate or muscle tension) be monitored and the information fed back to a client. Through this process, a client learns techniques to control the function, for example, learning to relax to slow the heart rate or decrease muscle tension.

- **Aversive conditioning** requires a client repeatedly to pair undesirable behavior(s) with aversive stimuli (for example, electric shocks, nausea-producing substances, or verbal insults) in order to stop the behavior(s). Mixing alcohol with a nausea-producing substance, resulting in an association between ingestion of alcohol and unpleasantness, is an example of aversive conditioning.

- When the learning technique of **modeling** (p. 68) is used to change behavior, a client watches another person perform the client's feared behavior(s), and with encouragement from the therapist, the client copies that performance.

- Particularly in institutions, therapists may establish what is known as a **token economy,** in which **tokens** are given as rewards (an operant procedure) to encourage (shape) behaviors such as getting out of bed and dressing. A sufficient number of tokens may then be traded for rewards such as food and movies.

Cognitive therapies. **Cognitive therapies** use learning principles involving cognition to change maladaptive thoughts, beliefs, and feelings that contribute to emotional and behavioral problems.

- **Cognitive therapy for depression** was originally developed by Aaron Beck, who suggested that depressed people view themselves and the world around them negatively because of distortions in thinking. These distortions are classified as **selective perception** (focusing on only bad events), **overgeneralization** (allowing one discouraging event to be generalized to a negative interpretation of all events), and **all-or-none thinking** (a tendency to see all events as entirely good or entirely bad). A client is helped to recognize and to change these maladaptive cognitive behaviors.

- **Rational-emotive therapy (ET)**, developed by Albert Ellis, is one of the best known cognitive therapies and is based on the premise that many problems arise from irrational thinking. People are thought to become unhappy and to develop self-defeating habits because of faulty beliefs. An example might be a person who has a need to be perfect in all actions and feels dismal after failure. The therapy helps a client to understand the irrationality and the consequences of such a way of thinking, reduce anxiety in a stressful situation, and learn to substitute more effective problem-solving tactics.

Feminist therapy. **Feminist therapy** emerged as a challenge to the mental health establishment's role in maintaining social inequities between men and women and other majority and minority groups. Feminist therapists oppose the use of both gender-role stereotypes, which support cultural beliefs in male superiority and female inferiority, and any type of discrimination on the basis of age, ethnic group, or sexual orientation. Although these therapists use a variety of therapeutic techniques, they always consider the role of society in creating discrimination and thus contributing to a client's problems in daily life. Therapists are encouraged to understand their own social biases and the manner in which those biases operate in the therapeutic process.

Group therapies. **Group therapies** apply therapeutic principles, except for psychoanalysis, to a group of people. Although in group therapy a therapist's involvement with a single client is not as extensive as in individual therapy, clients learn from the experiences of other clients and from their reactions to one another. Group activities may include **self-help** as well as **support** from and **confrontation** by other group members. Some groups focus on particular strategies. This procedure is usually less expensive than individual therapy.

- In **family therapy,** all family members participate, individually and as a group. The process allows destructive relationships and interaction styles to be identified and changed. A family is considered to be any group of people who are committed to one another's well-being, preferably for life.

- **Marital therapy** assists husbands and wives to work together as a couple to solve their problems and has as a major goal the development of realistic expectations about a marriage relationship.

- **Self-help groups,** so called because they include no professional therapist, consist of people who voluntarily assemble on a regular basis to discuss topics of interest. Group members, including a group leader, provide support to help individual members with problems. Such groups, because they use community resources and are consequently relatively inexpensive, are important for many people. Alcoholics Anonymous (AA) and Take Off Pounds Sensibly (TOPS) are two of the best known self-help groups.

- In **sensitivity groups,** participants engage in activities that encourage individual self-awareness and awareness and trust of others.

- **Encounter groups** help members confront emotion-laden experiences openly and without distortion. Members of the group identify annoying behaviors of individual members, such as incessant bragging or continual "put-downs" of others, and openly confront the person for such behavior. The group allows the participants to feel free to express true feelings about each other.

- In **psychodrama,** an early group approach, an individual acts out incidents similar to those that cause real-life problems. The technique uses **role-reversal,** with the client assuming the role of the person creating difficulties, as an aid in understanding life's problems.

Community psychology. Community psychology practitioners seek to reach out to the community to provide services such as community health centers and especially to effect social change through planning, prevention, early intervention, evaluation, research, and the empowerment of individuals. A major aim of the effort is to strengthen existing social support networks and to stimulate the formation of new networks to meet challenges. A key idea in community psychology is **empowerment,** helping people to use existing skills and to develop motivation to acquire new knowledge in order to gain control over their lives.

- **Crisis intervention centers,** such as those that assist rape victims, help people deal with short-term, stressful situations resulting from a crisis. The centers also help in community education about the problems encountered and, based on those problems, often advocate changes in community institutions and organizations.

- **Community halfway houses** serve as treatment facilities and residences for those who have been released from a mental hospital or prison and for those who are considered to be at risk of needing mental hospital care. They are run by a nonprofessional staff under the supervision of a professional. The residents work in the community but receive support and some supervision in daily activities.

Biomedical Therapies

Biomedical therapies are physiological interventions that focus on the reduction of symptoms associated with psychological disorders. Three procedures used are drug therapies, electroconvulsive (shock) treatment, and psychosurgery.

Drug therapies. Drug therapies **(psychopharmacotherapy)**, which rely on medication for the treatment of mental disorders, are sometimes used by professionals with appropriate medical or pharmacological training in conjunction with psychotherapy. Therapeutic drugs for psychological problems fall into three major groups. Commonly used types of each and their generic names, trade names (and chemical names) follow.

- **Antianxiety drugs** (mild tranquilizers) are used to relieve anxiety.

  — **benzodiazepines:** Valium (diazepam), Xanax (alprazolam), Librium (chlordiazepoxide)

  — **barbiturates:** Miltown (meprobamate)

  — **hypnotics:** Halcion (triazolam), Dalmane (flurazepam)

  When people discontinue these drugs after taking them for a long time, they may suffer **rebound anxiety** (a reoccurrence of the earlier anxiety).

- **Antipsychotic drugs** (also called **major tranquilizers** or **neuroleptics**) are used primarily to treat schizophrenia and to reduce psychotic symptoms such as hyperactivity, hallucinations, delusions, and mental confusion.

  — **phenothiazines:** Mellaril (thioridazine), Thorazine (chlorpromazine), Prolixin (fluphenazine)

  — **butyrophenones:** Haldol (haloperidol)

Pharmacotherapy treatment may produce side effects such as drowsiness, constipation, and dry mouth. Antipsychotic drug treatment may cause a severe and lasting problem called **tardive dyskinesia,** a neurological disorder characterized by involuntary writhing and ticlike movements of the mouth, tongue, face, hands, or feet.

- **Antidepressant drugs** are used to elevate mood and to treat depressions. Three principal classes of antidepressants are

  — **tricyclics:** Trofranil (imipramine), Elavil (amitriptyline)

  — **monoamine oxidase (MAO) inhibitors:** Nardil (phenelzine), Marplan (isocarboxazid)

  — **selective serotonin reuptake inhibitors (SSRIs):** Zoloft (sertraline), Prozac (fluoxetine), Paxil (paroxetine). Some patients taking Prozac have developed suicidal tendencies.

- **Lithium (lithium carbonate)** is used to treat patients with bipolar mood disorders to control mood swings. The drug may have dangerous side effects, however, such as kidney and thyroid damage.

Electroconvulsive therapy. In **electroconvulsive therapy (ECT),** a therapeutic procedure developed in the 1930s before many of today's psychopharmacological drugs had been developed, an electric shock is given to lightly anesthetized patients to produce a brief cortical seizure. The shock is administered to one side or sometimes to both sides of the brain through electrodes placed over the temporal lobes. The electric current produces a brief convulsive seizure during which the patient becomes unconscious. ECT was widely used in the 1940s and 1950s; its use has declined, but not entirely stopped, as treatment with new drugs has grown in favor. While favorable results with ECT have been reported for some cases, marked controversy still exists concerning whether it is effective and whether it produces permanent intellectual impairment.

Psychosurgery. Psychosurgery, a surgical procedure designed to change psychological or behavioral reactions (also developed in the 1930s), is more controversial than ECT and is rarely used today. The most widely used was **lobotomy,** also called **prefrontal lobotomy,** which requires the severing of nerve pathways linking the cerebral cortex to the lower brain centers as a means of controlling a patient's violent or aggressive tendencies. However, even if the procedure is successful in controlling violence, it often produces other side effects. More recently, different and technically more sophisticated (but still very experimental) surgical procedures for controlling some mental disorders are being investigated (such as electrical stimulation of a brain area to treat Parkinson's disease).

Institutionalization

The process of **institutionalizing** the mentally ill began in the sixteenth century and continues today. New drug treatments, along with overcrowding and bad conditions in some hospitals, has led to **deinstitutionalization** in recent years. Formerly hospitalized patients are now treated with psychoactive drugs and other therapies in their homes and communities. Community health centers have been designed to provide a variety of services, including short-term inpatient and outpatient care as well as consultation, education, and prevention programs.

Social psychologists study the thoughts, feelings, and actions of people in social situations or, conversely, the influence of others on those thoughts, feelings, and actions. Social psychology deals with group behavior as well as the behavior of individuals within groups.

Attitudes

Attitudes are lasting patterns of beliefs and opinions which predispose reactions to objects, events, and people. Attitudes may also serve as brief composites of one's beliefs. (For example, through generalization, those who fear their father may initially experience fear upon meeting any older man.) Attitudes may be quantified by using **self-report measures** or **attitude scales** such as the popular **Likert scale** (named after Robert Likert) in which subjects are asked how strongly they agree or disagree on each topic. A total attitude score is derived by summing the measures. Another measurement approach employs **covert measures,** observations of behaviors such as facial expressions, voice tone, and body language. (The latter measures may lack validity, as people monitor such covert behaviors in some situations.) Assessment strategies also include measures of **physiological arousal,** for example, by means of a **facial electromyograph (EMG)** (to record facial muscle activity) or an **electroencephalograph (EEG)** (to measure brain activity). Such measures, which can detect responses a person may be trying to conceal, are obtained as a subject hears verbal material designed to produce arousal and with which they might agree or disagree.

Attitude components. Attitudes consist of cognitive, behavioral, and affective components.

- The **cognitive component** is made up of the **beliefs** of an individual about the object of an attitude, for example, the belief that all old people are senile.

- The **behavioral component** consists of a predisposition to respond in a certain way to the object of the attitude, for example, talking to an old person as if talking to a child.

- The **affective component** refers to emotions aroused by the object of the attitude, for example, always feeling sorry for an older person.

Attitude formation. Attitude formation occurs through classical conditioning, operant conditioning, and modeling (observational learning) (p. 60). Advertising relies to a great extent upon modeling when it shows a famous person using and liking a product. Some theories describing the formation of attitudes follow.

- **Balance theory,** proposed by Fritz Heider, is based on the premise that people try to maintain consistency in their attitudes. If an attitude inconsistency occurs, such as believing all old people to be senile but meeting an older person who is intelligent and mentally active, the person who holds the attitude tries to reestablish consistency either by changing the attitude or changing the perception of the older person as intelligent.

- Proponents of **reactance theory** contend that attitudes are influenced by restrictions on behavior, to which people react. The extent of reaction is related to a person's perception of the relative importance of the behavior. If a behavior, although restricted, is not considered important, there is little reaction. If, however, the activity is considered important and the restriction unjust, then the restriction itself makes the activity even more attractive. For example, if a teenager wants to date a person her parents disapprove of and forbid her to see, she might find that person even more desirable as a result and date on the sly.

- **Cognitive dissonance theory** (developed by Leon Festinger) states that an unpleasant physiological state often exists when two cognitions are incompatible with one another. The incompatibility creates tensions, which a person tries to relieve. For example, a student who advocates honesty but who does cheat on an examination must either alter her or his self-concept or rationalize the cheating behavior to reduce tension.

- **Self-perception theory** (introduced by Daryl Bem) proposes that people infer their attitudes on the basis of observing their own behavior(s). A usually honest student who does cheat on an exam may infer the attitude from the behavior by thinking, "Being first is more important than honesty to me" or "I believe that the end justifies the means."

Attitude change. **Attitude change** may occur through the use of **persuasion,** the process of intentionally attempting to alter an attitude. Persuasion includes variations in the **source** (origin of the message), the **message** (information transmitted), and the **receiver** of the message. Persuasion is likely to be more effective if an individual likes rather than dislikes the source and if the source is viewed as trustworthy and credible. The manner in which the message is presented (for example, in every-day language rather than technical terminology) as well as the characteristics of the receiver (for example, being a teenager rather than middle-aged) affect the ease of attitude change.

Attributions

Attributions are inferences generated by people when they try to explain reasons for events, the behavior of others, and their own behavior. Attributions may be **internal (dispositional)**, based on something within a person, or **external (situational)**, based on something outside a person. A student who wins an art contest may decide it is because of ability (internal attribution) or because the judges are friends of her or his parents (external attribution). The tendency to overuse internal attributions (such as blaming an adolescent driver rather than road conditions for a car accident) is called the **fundamental attribution error.** Another type of attribution error, called **self-serving bias,** is described as the predisposition to attribute successes to abilities and efforts and failures to external, situational causes. Bernard Weiner, in his study of attributions made concerning success or failure, suggested that both internal and external attributions may be based on **stability** (that is, an internal factor may be deemed either stable or unstable) and **controllability** (the factor may be deemed either controllable or uncontrollable).

Social Influence

The term **social influence** refers to the ways in which external factors alter behavior. Several types of social influence are discussed below.

- **Conformity** is changing one's behavior because of perceived pressure. Solomon Asch conducted a famous study on conformity in which seven subjects were asked to judge line lengths. Six of the subjects were confederates of the experimenter and gave wrong responses, and on many occasions, the real subject conformed and also gave wrong responses.

- In Stanley Milgram's well-known study of **obedience to authority,** subjects were told that they were assisting in a learning experiment and were ordered to give other subjects (confederates of the experimenter) shocks when they made an incorrect response. Although shocks were not actually given, the real subjects were told that shock intensity increased as the experiment progressed. To the amazement of all, all the subjects (supposedly assisting the experimenter), even though they became agitated, continued to obey the experimenter and to administer shocks even at shock intensities they believed to be 300 volts. At that time, the supposed learner pounded the wall as though in pain, and 22% of the subjects refused to continue. Others, however, did continue and increased the intensity to 450 volts.

- The subject of **bystander intervention** became of interest after a cocktail waitress was brutally murdered on a New York street. People heard her scream, but no one came to her aid. Research was conducted to determine factors that might lead to bystander intervention or to bystander apathy, as occurred in the New York case. Working on this topic, Bibb Latané and John Darley, concluded that people are more likely to receive help when they are alone rather than in a group and that the larger the group, the smaller the responsibility to intervene that bystanders feel. The cognitive model developed to explain bystander intervention (or a lack of it) includes the following concepts.

  —**audience inhibition,** a reluctance to act in front of others

  —**pluralistic ignorance,** an individual's interpretation that lack of action by others means that there is no emergency

  —**diffusion of responsibility,** allowing others to share and thus assume responsibility in the intervention process

Behavior in Groups

Behavior that occurs when two or more people interact is the subject of the study of **behavior in groups.** The presence of others may promote a variety of behavioral processes.

- The phenomenon of **social facilitation,** improved performance due to the presence of others, is believed to be due to a fear of evaluation as well as others' presence.

- **Social interference** (also referred to as **social loafing**) is decreased performance when working in a group. Robert Zajonc found that social facilitation occurs more frequently if a task is simple or well learned and social interference when a task is complex or unpracticed.

- **Group polarization** is a process whereby an individual's pre-existing attitudes are strengthened as a consequence of group discussion that supports those attitudes. One explanation of the phenomenon is that in a group individual responsibility becomes diffused because an individual cannot be held responsible for the group's decisions.

- **Groupthink** is the phenomenon of group members supporting one another and seeking agreement and group cohesiveness rather than realistically appraising alternatives. Because the practice discourages disagreement, unpopular but important information may be ignored in such a group's decision making.

Aggression

Aggression is behavior, verbal or physical, intended to physically hurt or harm in some other way another person or thing. Whether aggression is manifested by individuals or groups (including nations), it is the most destructive force in social relations and consequently an important social issue. A major concern in either individual or group aggression is its origin.

- **Biology** has a role in aggression. **Genetic** influences play a major part in some aggression, as evidenced in animals specifically bred to exhibit such behavior. Studies of identical twins have frequently shown that if one twin exhibits aggressive behavior, the other often does so as well. Aggression may also have a neural basis; aggressive behavior has been produced in animals through electrical stimulation of parts of the brain.

- Konrad Lorenz, an ethologist, proposed that aggression arises from **instincts** and that such instincts help members of a species maximize the use of food, space, and other resources. Other biologists have studied the aggression produced by exposing the nervous system to **chemicals** (drugs, such as alcohol) or **hormones** (such as testosterone).

- **Learning** theorists such as John Dollard have suggested that frustration of goal-directed behavior leads to aggression (the **frustration-aggression hypothesis**). Imagine your response, for example, if after you've stood in line for hours to get game tickets, the person just ahead of you gets the last ones.

- **Social learning,** acquisition of behaviors by watching others, is believed to function in learning aggressive behaviors. Research has shown that children model aggressive behavior, and data exist that suggest that exposure to media violence increases a person's tendency to be aggressive. Domestic violence (in which a person is beaten by her or his spouse) is a serious modern social problem. Studies indicate that male abusers often come from families in which the mother was abused or have frequently observed other violence.

Prejudice

Prejudice is a negative attitude about members of a group. Prejudice translated into behavior is called **discrimination,** behaving differently, usually unfairly, toward group members. Prejudice often develops through **stereotypes,** fixed, simplistic (usually wrong) conceptions of traits, behaviors, and attitudes of a particular group of people. The widely practiced discrimination termed **sexism** is based on a **gender** stereotype that women are inferior.

Causes of prejudice. While the causes of prejudice are complex, the following have been suggested as methods of acquiring prejudiced beliefs.

- **social learning:** Children learn prejudice by watching parents and friends.

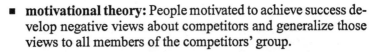
- **motivational theory:** People motivated to achieve success develop negative views about competitors and generalize those views to all members of the competitors' group.

- **personality theory:** People develop prejudices because of experiences during their development. For example, a person reared by a red-haired authoritarian woman who uses physical punishment may develop a prejudice against all women with red hair.

- **cognitive theory:** People conceptualize their world by using mental shortcuts to organize it, for example, by thinking such things as "all homeless people are alike."

Elimination of prejudice. Prejudice can be eliminated in several ways, including acquainting prejudiced people with a member of the group they are prejudiced against and teaching them to think rationally about such matters as status equality and changing social norms through desegregation.

Interpersonal Attraction

Interpersonal attraction, any of a variety of positive attitudes toward another person, can take many forms, including

- **affiliation:** wanting to be with another person

- **liking:** having a generally positive attitude toward another person

- **friendship:** a mutual liking between two people, their wanting to be together

- **love:** a process made up of intimacy, passion, and commitment

Robert Sternberg proposed a **triangular model of love** and described three components of love, **passion, intimacy,** and **decision/commitment,** which combine to create four types of love.

- **ideal (consummate) love:** (difficult to achieve) passion + intimacy + decision/commitment
- **romantic love:** intimacy + passion
- **companionate love:** intimacy + decision/commitment
- **fatuous love:** passion + decision/commitment

Altruism

Altruism is helping behavior (without expectation of extrinsic rewards and sometimes involving personal risk or sacrifice) that benefits individuals or society. Altruism originates, as does aggression, from biological components such as instincts, from learning through such methods as reinforcement, and through modeling of significant others.

Intelligence Tests

Intelligence is often defined as a measure of general mental ability. Of the standardized intelligence tests, those developed by David Wechsler are among those most widely used. Wechsler defined intelligence as "the global capacity to act purposefully, to think rationally, and to deal effectively with the environment." While psychologists generally agree with this definition, they don't agree on the **operational definition** of intelligence (that is, a statement of the procedures to be used to precisely define the variable to be measured) or how to accomplish its measurement.

Test construction. To be useful, tests, including intelligence tests, must be constructed using the established criteria of standardization, reliability, and validity.

- **Standardization** is the process of making uniform and objective both testing procedures and scoring procedures in order to obtain meaningful scores. Scores on standardized tests are interpreted in reference to scores obtained from a **standardization sample,** that is, scores from a comparable group of subjects tested under appropriate conditions.

- The term **reliability** refers to the consistency of results. Reliability of a test is determined by one of the following methods.

  — **test and retest reliability:** comparison of original test scores with retest scores

  — **alternate form reliability:** comparison of scores obtained on alternate forms of a test

  — **split-half reliability:** comparison of scores obtained on two halves of tests (such as scores on odd- versus even-numbered questions)

- The term **validity** refers to the extent that a test measures what it is supposed to measure. Types of validity include

  — **content validity:** the extent to which a test reflects a sample of the behavior to be measured

  — **predictive validity:** the extent to which a test can predict a person's behavior in another situation

  — **face validity:** how appropriate a test "appears" to be, just from the way the items read

  — **construct validity:** how well a test assesses the construct (for example, intelligence) for which it was designed

  — **concurrent validity:** how well the results of a test agree with those of a new test or a different form of the test measuring for the same construct (for example, intelligence)

Measures of intelligence.

- Sir Francis Galton, a pioneer in the measurement of **individual differences** in late nineteenth-century England, was particularly concerned with sensory responses (visual and auditory acuity and reaction times) and their relationship to differences in ability.

- Several **individual tests** have been used to test intelligence.

  — The **Binet-Simon intelligence scale,** developed by French psychologists Alfred Binet and Theodore Simon, was administered to children to evaluate their performance (**mental age**) at a given **chronological age.** The mental age/chronological age measure, called a **mental quotient,** was used to evaluate a child's learning potential.

  — Lewis Terman of Stanford University revised the Binet scale in 1916. The revised scale, called the **Stanford-Binet intelligence scale,** although it retained the concept of mental and chronological ages, introduced the concept of the **in-**

telligence quotient (IQ) arrived at by the following widely used formula, which allows comparison between children of different ages.

$$\text{intelligence quotient (IQ)} = \frac{\text{mental age}}{\text{chronological age}} \times 100$$

The 1986 revision of the test, the latest of several, varies the calculation so that the test is useful for adults as well as for children. An individual's score for correct answers is compared to a table of scores of test takers of the same age (with the average score always scaled to 100). Scores between 90 and 110 are labeled as "normal," above 130 as "superior," and below 70 as mentally deficient, or "retarded." The distribution of IQ scores approximates a normal (bell-shaped) curve (Figure 20).

The Normal IQ Distribution

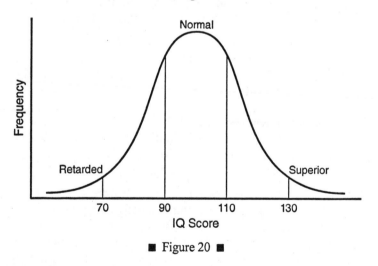

■ Figure 20 ■

—David Wechsler developed the **Wechsler Adult Intelligence Scale (WAIS)** in 1939, revised as the **WAIS-R.** Wechsler also developed the **Wechsler Intelligence Scale for Children (WISC),** revised as the **WISC-R.** The revised forms of these scales are still widely used. They contains two subscales, **verbal** and **performance,** which provide a **verbal IQ** and a **performance IQ;** the subscales are combined for the **total IQ.** Test score combinations may reveal other strengths and weaknesses to a skilled examiner.

Tests of aptitude and achievement. Group tests (such as the California Achievement Tests and the SAT, the Scholastic Assessment Test) are often used to measure **aptitude,** the capacity to learn (including both verbal and performance aptitudes) and **achievement,** what has been learned.

Ranges of intelligence scores. The two extremes of levels of intellectual functioning are known as developmentally disabled and gifted.

- Those identified as **mentally retarded** (sometimes described as **developmentally disabled**) have IQ scores of 70 or below. Severity of disability and corresponding IQ scores are mild (50 to 70), moderate (35 to 50), severe (20 to 35), and profound (below 20). Some, but not all, of the causes of mental retardation are known and include Down syndrome, a genetic disorder; phenylketonuria, a metabolic disorder; and developmental disability due to anoxia (lack of oxygen) during gestation.

- The **gifted** usually fall within the upper 2% to 3% of the IQ score distribution (between 130 and 145). Louis Terman's well-known longitudinal study of the gifted, which will not be complete until 2010, found that gifted children are generally superior to average-IQ peers in health, achievement, and adjustment to life stresses. Currently, gifted children are identified not only by IQ but also by superior potential in any of six areas: general intelligence, specific aptitudes (math, for example), creativity, leadership, performing arts, and athletics.

Other Concepts of Intelligence

Spearman's two-factor theory. Charles Spearman, using the statistical procedure called factor analysis, concluded in 1904 that intelligence is made up of two components: a **g-factor** (general intelligence) and **s-factors** (a collection of specific cognitive intellectual skills).

Thurstone's primary mental abilities. L. L. Thurstone proposed in 1938 that primary mental abilities fall into seven categories.

- **verbal comprehension** (V)
- **number** (N)
- **spatial relations** (S)
- **perceptual speed** (P)
- **word fluency** (W)
- **memory** (M)
- **inductive reasoning** (I), or **general reasoning** (R)

According to Thurstone, each ability can be measured separately, and the sum of the unique abilities composes intelligence.

Guilford's three-dimensional model. J. P. Guilford proposed three dimensions of mental ability:

- **operations:** the act of thinking
- **contents:** the terms used in thinking
- **products of thinking:** ideas

Each of these dimensions is subdivided (operations, for example, into such categories as evaluation, cognition, and memory). Combinations of the dimensions and subdivisions can lead to over 100 separate factors, many of which have been demonstrated experimentally.

Fluid and crystallized intelligence. Raymond Cattell and John Horn suggested that the g-factor should be divided into fluid intelligence and crystallized intelligence.

- **Fluid intelligence** consists of reasoning ability, memory capacity, and speed of information processing. It involves such skills as those requiring spatial and visual imagery and is generally believed to be much less affected by experience and education than is crystallized intelligence.

- **Crystallized intelligence** concerns the application of knowledge to problem solving. It includes abilities such as reasoning and verbal and numerical skills and is generally believed to be affected by experience and formal education.

The concepts of fluid and crystallized intelligence are still used by some psychologists, particularly in the area of aging.

Vernon's hierarchical model. Philip Vernon suggested that intelligence consists of factors and skills arranged hierarchically. The **cognitive factor,** at the top, is composed of two skills, **verbal/academic** and **practical/mechanical,** each of which is itself subdivided. (Verbal/academic, for example, includes such skills as vocabulary and verbal fluency.)

Sternberg's triarchic theory. Robert Sternberg was concerned with how intelligence is used, particularly in problem solving, as well the abilities it includes. The theory deals with

- **componential intelligence,** which includes components essential to acquisition of knowledge, use of problem-solving strategies and techniques, and use of metacognitive components for selecting a strategy and monitoring progress toward success

- **experiential intelligence,** which is reflected both in creatively dealing with new situations and then combining different experiences in insightful ways to solve novel problems

- **contextual intelligence,** which is reflected in the management of day-to-day affairs

Gardner's seven intelligences. Howard Gardner divided intelligence into seven abilities. Although the abilities are intrinsically equally important, their value in a particular culture may vary. For example, people who live off the land in a remote jungle are more likely to value bodily-kinesthetic abilities more than logical-mathematical abilities. Gardner's intelligences include

- **linguistic ability**
- **logical-mathematical ability**
- **spatial ability:** navigating spatially; forming, transforming, and using mental images
- **musical ability:** perceiving and creating rhythm and pitch patterns
- **bodily-kinesthetic ability:** motor coordination and movement skills
- **interpersonal ability:** understanding others
- **intrapersonal ability:** having self-understanding, a sense of identity

Memory, which is both a process and an entity, is the retention of information over a period of time. Of concern are the processes for putting information into memory (encoding), maintaining the coded information (storage), and getting the stored information back into consciousness (retrieval). Of concern also is forgetting (losing stored information or having difficulty or failure in retrieving it), which may occur because of problems in any of the three memory processes.

Hermann Ebbinghaus (1850–1909), a philosopher, applied the scientific method to the study of memory and, in a procedure involving the memorization of nonsense syllables, discovered an important relationship between the time spent learning and relearning information and level of retention, a relationship called the saving method. (Subjects who could relearn a brief list of words quickly were thought to have retained some memory of the list.) (See p. 177.) Frederic Bartlett (1886–1969) was interested in the number of trials required to memorize information. He argued that in remembering information, people often fill in the gaps by means of inferences about what *could* have been the case (a phenomenon that may occur in the so-called **false memory** of some eye witnesses, p. 179). These early, diverse approaches to the study of memory illustrate the diversity in the field in general.

Encoding

Encoding, the transformation as well as the transfer of information into a memory system, requires, in general, **selective attention,** the focusing of awareness on a particular set of stimuli or events. Information may also be encoded at different levels of processing. Consider, for example, the possible processing levels concerning a word projected briefly on a screen. **Shallow (structural)** processing focuses on the physical characteristics of the written word; **intermediate (phonemic)** processing focuses on phonemic encoding (the sound of the word); and **deep (semantic)** processing focuses on semantic encoding (the meaning of the word).

Encoding may be enhanced by means of

- **visual imagery:** formation of visual images of things to be remembered

- **elaboration:** developing an association/link to the topic to be remembered

- **relevance:** making the material to be remembered personally relevant

and through the following organizational procedures:

- **chunking:** organizing the material to be remembered into groups, as, for example, telephone numbers are arranged—(area code) (three digits) (four digits).

- **hierarchies:** grouping information to be remembered into categories and possibly into hierarchies consisting of major and minor concepts

Storage

Memory is **stored** by means of three memory systems: sensory memory, short-term memory, and long-term memory.

Sensory memory. **Sensory memory** preserves incoming sensory information (in its original sensory form) for only a fraction of a second. (A visual memory trace is called an **icon;** an auditory memory trace is called an **echo.**) **Sensory memory** extends the duration of the perception of stimuli long enough that they can be recognized, transformed (encoded), and relayed to conscious awareness.

Short-term memory. **Short-term memory (STM)** has a limited duration (15 to 30 seconds) and a limited capacity, believed to be about seven pieces of information. (In his 1956 study, George Miller spoke of the magical number of seven, plus or minus two.) It is thought that STM can be increased by using a tactic called **maintenance rehearsal** (rote recital of stored information).

Long-term memory. **Long-term memory (LTM)** has an unlimited capacity and a very long duration; it is virtually limitless. **Repetition** and **elaborative rehearsal** (manipulation of information by giving it meaning) are helpful techniques in storing information in LTM.
Endel Tulving divided LTM into

- **procedural memory:** retention of stimulus-response associations and patterns of procedural responses (such as skipping rope and riding a bicycle)

- **episodic memory:** memories of life events or experiences

- **semantic memory:** knowledge of words, symbols, or concepts and the rules for their manipulation or usage, such as in a language

Researchers have also identified another type of LTM, **metamemory,** which is knowledge of how memory systems work and how to use them in retrieving stored information.
The permanence of LTM is supported by such phenomena as **flashbulb memory,** the consistent and detailed recollection of a significant occurrence. For example, many Americans still remember what they were doing when Pearl Harbor was attacked in World War II.
Primacy and recency effects are phenomena also associated with LTM.

- Recall of information is enhanced when individuals have no information stored in STM and their attention to new stimuli is at its peak (a situation known as the **primacy effect**), as happens, for example, in more easily recalling words presented at the beginning of a list.

- Recall of the most recently presented information is also enhanced (a situation known as the **recency effect**), as happens, for example, in more easily recalling the words presented at the end of a list.

The plot of the likelihood of recalling items from a list is illustrated in the U-shaped curve (known as the **serial position curve**) illustrated in Figure 21.

The Serial Position Curve

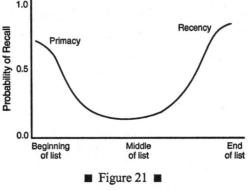

■ Figure 21 ■

Retrieval

Retrieval is the process of getting information out of memory. **Retrieval cues** are stimuli that can be used to help retrieve memories. **Priming** is the process of identifying traces (perhaps associations made at the time the memory was formed) that lead to a memory. Some researchers believe that recalling the **context** of the original experience assists in retrieval; others believe that recalling the mood associated with the memory formation, a process called **state-dependent learning,** is helpful. For example, a person who is feeling depressed might recall an event that occurred during a previous period of depression. Some people create mental pictures of an event or object, a process called **imagery,** to enhance retrieval. A few individuals employ an extremely detailed photographic visualization called **eidetic imagery.**

Forgetting

Forgetting is the loss or failure of memory. Hermann Ebbinghaus studied the relationship between ease of relearning (called **savings)** and the time between learning and relearning, which he expressed as a forgetting curve (Figure 22). He found that most forgetting occurs during the first nine hours after learning.

The Forgetting Curve

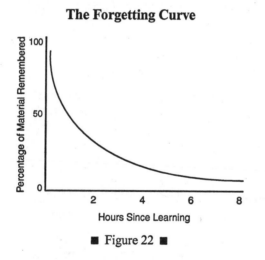

■ Figure 22 ■

Practice, both **massed** and **distributed** over time, also affects relearning forgotten material. Ebbinghaus also found that the more an individual rehearses a list of syllables, the better the syllables are recalled. (And as would be expected, given the primacy and recency effects, syllables near the beginning or end of a list are recalled best.) When graphed, the effect of practice results in a U-shaped curve similar to that in Figure 21.

Measures of retention. Memories may be retrieved in three ways.

- **recall:** remembering of previously learned information

  — **free recall:** recall of items in any order

  — **serial recall:** recall of items in the order in which they were learned

  — **paired associate recall:** recall of a second item based on a cue supplied by a first item

- **recognition:** identification of previously learned information (as, for example from a number of answer choices in a multiple-choice test)

- **reconstruction:** rebuilding of a scenario from certain remembered details

Reasons for forgetting.

- **Decay** is loss of information from memory as a consequence of the passage of time and lack of use. It has been suggested that memory is stored in **memory traces,** which disappear when not used for a long time.

- **Interference** is the confusion of one piece of information with another or the suppression of one in favor of another that was processed about the same time (as might happen, for example, if a student takes a Spanish lesson one period and a French lesson the next).

  — **Proactive interference** occurs if previously learned material interferes with learning of new material.

  — **Retroactive interference** occurs if learning of new material interferes with the ability to recall previously learned material.

- **Amnesia** is the inability to remember events from the past because of a psychological trauma (**psychogenic amnesia**) or a physiological trauma (**organic amnesia**), such as brain damage resulting from a blow to the head. The memory loss is usually limited to a specific period.

—**Retrograde amnesia** is the inability to remember happenings that preceded the traumatic event producing the amnesia.

—**Anterograde amnesia** is the inability to remember happenings that occur after a traumatic event.

- People sometimes forget things because they find them too unpleasant to think about. Such an occurrence is called **motivated forgetting.** Sigmund Freud attributed many memory failures, particularly involving painful childhood experiences, to **repression** (the process of keeping disturbing thoughts or feelings relegated to the unconscious). The repressed material can sometimes be recalled through free association or hypnosis. The recovery of supposedly repressed memories, such as those of childhood sexual abuse, is controversial. Some psychologists, such as Elizabeth Loftus, have called some of the recovered information **false memories** and suggested that sometimes such information has been implanted by the client's therapist.

Eyewitness testimony. Eyewitness testimony is the courtroom recall of a real-life situation. Studies have shown that eyewitnesses sometimes recall events incorrectly or identify the wrong people. In addition, memories may be embellished after the fact, particularly if a person has a stake in the outcome, but although the memories seemingly improve with time, they may be less rather than more accurate. The reliability of such embellished memories is controversial as is the use of hypnosis to improve memory retrieval.

Biological Substrates in Memory

Although much information exists on the connection between memory and biology, it is far from complete. At the neuron level, a deficiency of the neurotransmitter **acetylcholine** is a factor in the dementia (memory disorder) known as Alzheimer's disease (administration of the neurotransmitter has slowed the disease's progress but not prevented it). Reduced levels of the neurotransmitter **glutamate** have also been associated with the disorder. **Serotonin,** another neurotransmitter, is also thought to be important in memory functioning. Eric Kandel and James Schwartz, in a study of sea snails, found that **serotonin** is released as they learn. At the structural level, damage to the **hippocampus,** part of the limbic system, has been associated with memory difficulties.

Cognitive psychology is devoted to the study of mental processes used in **cognition** (thinking, remembering, and using language), which involves processing, understanding, and communicating information through the use of images, concepts, language, and problem solving.

Images

Images, mental, nonverbal representations of sensory experiences, affect our thinking and learning, particularly when dealing with physical skills and certain nonverbal material such as mathematical formulas. For example, the image we hold of a champion's superb golf stokes may govern our own attempts to develop similar skills.

Concepts

Concepts, the mental categories used to organize events and objects, are often arranged in hierarchical order from general to more specific—for example, organism, animal, vertebrate, quadruped, dog, collie. Such categories help people to understand new information and to plan—for example, by dividing available time into periods for study, class attendance, recreation, and so forth. People tend to use a **prototype,** a model of a concept, to typify members of a particular category. The prototype any particular individual uses depends on that individual's experience. Your prototype of "dog," for example, might be a long-haired, medium-size, long-muzzled, black and white, tail-wagging animal, and you would tend to classify dogs that you encounter as in various ways being the same as or different from your prototypical dog.

Theories of concept formation.

- The term **mediation theory** refers to the process used in forming connections between things previously not connected.

- The **hypothesis-testing theory** considers concept formation to be an active process in which people acquire information by generating hypotheses about stimuli, testing the hypotheses, and accepting them or discarding them and formulating others.

Language

Language is a system of communication using gestures, sounds, or written symbols that have significance for those who use the language and follow its rules. In speech, **phonemes** are the smallest units of sound in a language, and although they individually have no meaning, they acquire it when combined. For example, the phonemes *k* and *r* alone convey no meaning (other than that they are letters), but together they sound like *car,* which is a meaningful sound in the English language.

Semantics. The term **semantics** refers to the study of meaning in a language. The smallest unit of meaning in spoken language is called a **morpheme,** which in many instances is itself a word. The word *overcoat* is composed of two morphemes, *over* and *coat*. Language rules govern the combination of morphemes to create meaning; *overcoat,* for example, means something different than does *coatover.*

Sentences. Language rules also dictate **syntax,** how morphemes are put together to form **sentences,** groups of words that make meaningful statements. **Pragmatics** is the study of language as used in particular situations, which may affect its meaning. Consider the statement, "What a wonderful day!" and its various meanings if the sun is shining, if the rain is pouring down, and if the speaker has just received a traffic ticket.

Acquisition of language. B. F. Skinner believed that language acquisition, an important development in childhood, occurs because of reinforcement, that is, because childrens' parents or other caregivers reward them when their initially random sounds most resemble speech. Linguist Noam Chomsky contested Skinner's approach and proposed the well-known, but controversial, theory that children have an innate neural mechanism called a **language acquisition device (LAD)** (not yet discovered), which allows them to master language.

Developmental psychologists have subsequently documented the general process of language acquisition, which is usually thought to progress through the stages shown in Table 7.

LANGUAGE DEVELOPMENT	
Approximate Age	**Language Response**
4 months	Babbling—a variety of sounds, often repeated
10 months	Babbling that includes language used in the household
12 to 18 months	Single words (sometimes one word has a variety of meanings—**holophrastic speech**)
18 to 24 months	Two-word statements (often a noun and a verb—**telegraphic speech**)
30+ months	More complex sentences, greater vocabulary, rapid language expansion

■ Table 7 ■

Problem Solving

Steps in problem solving.

- **Problem interpretation** involves defining a problem and assigning it to a category. For example, defining the problem of how to pay for a college education would involve arriving at what the total costs will be including tuition, books, lab fees, housing, transportation, and so forth, in order to have a clear idea of the exact dimensions of the problem.

- **Evaluation of solutions,** the process of deciding on a strategy to solve a problem, may be accomplished by

  — **trial and error:** guessing or randomly trying an approach

  — **information retrieval:** retrieval of pertinent information from long-term memory; for example, recalling what a friend told you about her success in combining student loans and money earned from a part-time job to pay her expenses

  — **algorithms:** the methodical development of a step-by-step method to solve a problem; for example, creating a spreadsheet detailing plans for income-producing activities and projected expenses for each year of college

  — **heuristics:** rules of thumb to deal with a problem, sometimes based on information easily available in memory. For example, you might believe that since you've often heard that college funds are always available to students if they're willing to search them out, such funds will necessarily be available to you. You may, however, be inaccurate in your judgment if the information you've recalled is inaccurate.

A well-known heuristic tactic is called **means/ends analysis.** The process requires the identification of discrepancies that exist between a current situation and the achievement of a goal and then making changes that will reduce the differences. Another tactic is the **formation of subgoals,** the development of intermediate steps necessary to solve a problem. In some cases, it helps to **work backward** from the solution. This heuristic procedure requires consideration of the goal, conceptualization of steps necessary to solve the problem, and then accomplishing the steps nearest the goal first. For example, in planning for college, the student first chooses the college, then determines what the costs will be, then selects a job or prepares for getting a job that will allow that amount to be earned or first determines what the college's entrance requirements are and then plans for all of those to be met, and so forth.

Obstacles to solving problems.

- Although **arousal** (motivation) is necessary for problem solving, **high arousal** is detrimental to the process. Relaxation techniques can help to reduce such arousal and increase problem-solving efficiency.

- A **mental set,** a predisposition to approach problems in a certain fashion, can be helpful or harmful, depending on the set. For example, the set to do all homework before watching evening TV may be more likely to result in academic achievement than the reverse set of TV/study.

- **Functional fixedness** is the tendency to view an object or an activity in only one way—for example, seeing mathematics as a subject to be feared rather than as one that simply requires the learning of rules to solve problems and that is necessary to career development.

Aids in solving problems.

- To establish **expertise** is to establish the knowledge necessary to solve a problem—for example, by reading the chapter in the psychology text before attempting to answer the questions at the end of it.

- **Insight** is the sudden perception of the relationship between the components of a problem—for example, suddenly thinking of the word that fits the spaces in a crossword puzzle.

Decision Making

At least two procedures are used in **decision making,** choosing between possible solutions to a problem.

- In the **compensatory process,** all possible solutions are evaluated based on certain desirable features, which may overshadow certain undesirable ones.

- In the **noncompensatory process,** possible solutions are eliminated in a step-by-step process based on how well they meet *all* criteria—for example, cost, availability, and longevity.

Risky decisions are those made in the face of considerable uncertainty about the outcome of the decision. For example, although statistically the odds of winning a lottery are small, people still make the risky decision to participate. If they calculated the probability that their lottery ticket would be the winning one, the risk would be clear, but such decisions often rest on other than logical bases. Deciding to buy or not buy the lottery ticket can be affected by the way the decision maker frames the choice: "Oh, you spend only a dollar a week on the lottery, but you may make millions" vs. "For the $52 a year the lottery costs, I could buy some decent shoes; the chances of winning are only one in two million anyway."

Psychologists deal with a broad array of populations and must take into account differences in population characteristics when making predictions about behavior. If certain such characteristics are used inappropriately in making judgments, however, prejudice can result, and acting on prejudicial judgments leads to such discriminations as **sexism, racism,** and **ageism.** Psychologists are working to identify and hope to eliminate the bases for making inappropriate judgments concerning gender, cultural, racial, and age differences.

Gender

While in conversational English the term **gender** has come to refer to the biological characteristic of being female or male, in psychology, the term refers more inclusively to the social and cultural dimensions of being one sex or the other. **Gender identity** concerns individuals' perception of themselves as and identification with being female or male. A **Gender role** is the set of societal expectations that dictates how an individual of a gender should behave, think, and feel. During the past century, perception of all three aspects of gender have changed, particularly that of gender roles.

Biological factors. Although sex is determined by the presence of two X chromosomes or one X and one Y chromosome (p. 32), early in development, male and female fetuses are similar. Testes of males begin to differentiate around the seventh week after conception and ovaries of females around the twelfth week. Testes begin to secrete testosterone, which influences the development of the male sex organs.

Cognitive factors.

- The **cognitive development theory** contends that because children consistently hear themselves called "boy" or "girl," they begin to conceive of themselves as being of one sex or the other. Ultimately, from such interactions, children develop a conception of attitudes toward and behavioral expectations concerning that gender.

- The **gender schema theory** concerns the development of an internal schema, or mental framework, which organizes and directs the behavior of an individual as a male or female. For example, the gender schema of being female might include the proposition "I am a girl, so I play with dolls, not trucks."

Social factors. A society's treatment of one gender is often different from its treatment of the other, even from the time a child is born—for example "blue for boys and pink for girls." **Social learning theory** contends that children learn to behave in ways they are expected to behave as male or female by observing and imitating behaviors of people of their gender.

Gender roles. In the process of social learning, a child begins to learn her or his appropriate **gender role,** the sum of the behaviors society expects of females and of males. Gender roles vary in different cultures and have changed with time. Only recently has the role of "mother" been associated with that of "breadwinner" as well as that of "homemaker and mother." Although the term **androgyny** in popular usage often refers only to a combination of masculine and feminine physical characteristics, it is now frequently used specifically to describe an individual who displays both masculine and feminine characteristics of any kind that are deemed desirable, such as those shown by a man who engages in rough wrestling matches and yet tenderly holds and feeds a baby.

The psychology of gender. Courses on the **psychology of women** are now part of the curriculum at all major universities, and feminist scholars have reviewed the contributions made by women world-wide. Concomitantly, prejudice toward and discrimination against females at all developmental stages and both past and present (such as evidenced by treatment in classrooms and differences in salary) have been identified with the hope of ending them. Women of lower socio-economic status and of ethnic backgrounds different from that of the majority (in the United States, especially black women) have been particularly oppressed. Courses on the **psychology of gender** examine the role of gender in human behavior and the development of attitudes.

Culture and Race

Cultural and **racial diversity** may lead some individuals and societies to form prejudices about members of a particular culture or race and to practice discrimination. The term **culture** refers to ideas, behaviors, beliefs, and traditions shared by a large group of people and transmitted between generations. While cultural differences may also include racial differences, much diversity exists within one culture and within one race.

Race is genetically determined and refers to one's ancestry. **Ethnicity,** which refers to people's common traits, background, and allegiances (developed because of culture or religion), is learned from family, friends, and experiences. Only a small percentage of human genetic variation is due to racial differences; much more variation occurs between individuals within such groups. Psychologists are interested in identifying group differences (cultural diversity) as well as individual differences because that knowledge helps in understanding behavior.

Since all humans can learn and adapt, it is hoped that acceptance and understanding can replace prejudice and discrimination. To help in achieving this goal, the educational system has introduced courses on and disseminated information about cultural diversity and has included more faculty members of the less prevalent (minority) races and cultures. Cultures vary widely in their rules for acceptable and expected behavior as well as in the ways they guide the development of the individual. Knowing people from different cultures is one of the most effective ways of combating the formation of negative stereotypes and the development of prejudice. Courses on the **psychology of racism** examine the major terms and issues in psychology that pertain to race and racism in the United States and the general principles of racism that are universal.

Age

Ageism is prejudice against the elderly and the discrimination based on aging. Many myths exist about the capabilities of older people, especially older women, myths that lead to ill-founded stereotypes. Particularly in the United States, ageism persists in the job market and in the way older people are treated, both in real life and in the media. It is predicted that by the year 2030 one in five Americans will be elderly; more than 8 million will be 85 and over, and most of them will be women. Unless the problem of ageism is addressed, it will be an increasingly serious and far-reaching problem.

Psychologists who study adult development, as well as those in related disciplines such as gerontology, work toward an understanding of the aging process, understanding arising from data based on fact rather than stereotypes and myths.

APPENDIX

Statistics

Statistics is a branch of mathematics that provides procedures for the organization and analysis of data. Psychologists often use both descriptive statistics and inferential statistics, discussed below. Various measurement scales are used to categorize statistical data into meaningful and comparable form.

Measurement Scales

The type of data collected determines the appropriate measurement scale, and the measurement scale, in turn, determines the appropriate statistical procedure for analyzing particular data and drawing conclusions from that data. Each type of measurement scale has a specific use.

Nominal scales. **Nominal scales** are composed of sets of categories in which objects are classified. For example, a nominal scale dealing with household pets might include the categories dogs, cats, birds, and fish. Data used in the construction of a nominal scale are **frequency data,** the *number* of subjects in each category (in this case, the number of animals for each type of pet).

Ordinal scales. **Ordinal scales** indicate the *order* of the data according to some criterion. For example, a researcher might ask people to rank their preference for types of household pets, with 1 as the most preferred and 4 as the least preferred (resulting in, perhaps, 1-dogs, 2-cats, 3-birds, 4-fish). Ordinal scales tell nothing about the distance between units of the scale (for example, although dogs may be preferred to cats, no information is available about the extent of that preference) and supply information only about order of preference.

Interval scales. **Interval scales** have equal distances between scale units and permit statements to be made about those units as compared to other units (that is, one unit may be a certain number of units higher or lower than another), but they do not allow conclusions that one unit is a particular multiple of another because on interval scales there is no zero. That is, the scale does not allow for the complete absence of the phenomenon being measured. For example, if you refer to the interval scale used on a thermometer, you can say that 88 degrees is 2 degrees higher than 86 degrees, but you cannot accurately say that 88 degrees is twice as hot as 44 degrees because there is never a situation of no heat at all. (The zero on a thermometer doesn't indicate a complete lack of heat, only one more unit on the scale, which continues downward.) Interval scales, then, permit a statement of "more than" or "less than" but not of "how many times more."

Ratio scales. **Ratio scales** have equal distances between scale units as well as an absolute zero. If you're measuring the height of two trees and tree A is 36 inches tall and tree B is 72 inches tall, you can accurately say that B is twice as tall as A. There is a condition of zero height. Most measures encountered in daily living are based on a ratio scale.

Continuous and discontinuous scales. Measures may also be categorized according to continuity and discontinuity. A **continuous scale** is one in which the variable under consideration can assume an infinite number of values. A person's height, for example, might be expressed in an infinite number of ways, ranging from feet, to inches, to tenths of inches, to hundredths of inches, and so forth according to how small or large a measurement one wants to make. On the other hand, **discontinuous,** or **discrete, scales** express the measurement of the variable under consideration in a finite number of ways, as, for example, in a frequency distribution such as the number of students in a psychology department or the number of players on a team.

Descriptive Statistics

Descriptive statistics employs a set of procedures that make it possible to meaningfully and accurately summarize and describe samples of data. In order for one to make meaningful statements about psychological events, the variable or variables involved must be organized, measured, and then expressed as quantities. Such measurements are often expressed as measures of central tendency and measures of variability.

Organization of data. Graphical representation of data is typically the first organizational step. Frequency distributions, histograms, and/or frequency polygons are usually prepared in this process.

- A **frequency distribution,** often the first organizational step, is an ordered arrangement of all variables, which shows the number of occurrences in each category. Table 8 shows a frequency distribution concerning how much time students spent studying for an exam. Note that the total number tallied (counted) in each category by the researcher equals the number listed in the frequency column.

FREQUENCY DISTRIBUTION OF HOURS STUDIED FOR AN EXAM			
Hours Studied	Tally	Frequency	Total Hours Studied*
10	I	1	10
9	III	3	27
8	IIII	4	32
7	JHT	5	35
6	JHT III	8	48
5	JHT II	7	35
4	JHT	5	20
3	IIII	4	12
2	II	2	4
1	I	1	1
0		0	
		N = 40	Σ = 224

* total hours studied = hours studied × frequency
mean = 224/40 = 5.6, median = 6, mode = 6

■ Table 8 ■

Such a frequency distribution can be presented graphically as a frequency histogram or frequency polygon.

- **Frequency histograms** are bar graphs. Figure 23 shows a frequency histogram derived from the data in the frequency distribution in Table 8. The frequency (number of students) determined from the tally is the ordinate (vertical, or Y, axis), and the number of hours studied is the abscissa (horizontal, or X, axis). Each one-hour interval is presented sequentially, and the height of each bar represents the number of students who studied that number of hours.

Frequency Histogram: Hours Studied for an Exam

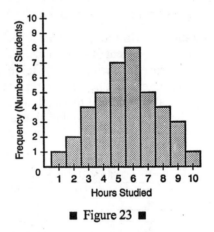

■ Figure 23 ■

- **Frequency polygons** are graphs in which the frequency of occurrence of the variable measured is shown by using connected points rather than bars. Figure 24 shows, in a frequency polygon, the same data displayed in Figure 23. (Note that if the

midpoints of each of the bars in Figure 23 were connected, the
result would be this frequency polygon.)

Frequency Polygon: Hours Studied for an Exam

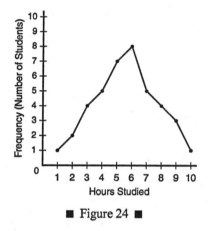

■ Figure 24 ■

Measures of central tendency. The three **measures of central tendency,** the mean, median, and mode, describe a distribution of data
and are an index of the average, or typical, value of a distribution of
scores.

- The **mean,** the arithmetic average of all scores under consideration, is computed by dividing the sum of the scores by the
number of scores. Based on the data in Table 8,

$$\frac{224}{40} = 5.6 \text{ hours} = \begin{array}{l} \text{mean number of hours} \\ \text{studied for the exam} \end{array}$$

- The **median** is the point at which 50% of the observations fall
below and 50% above or, in other words, the middle number
of a set of numbers arranged in ascending or descending order.
(If the list includes an even number of categories, the median
is the arithmetic average of the middle two numbers.) Based on
the data in Table 8, the full list of each student's study hours

would be written 10, 9, 9, 9, 8, 8, 8, 8, and so on. If the list were written out in full, it would be clear that the middle two numbers of the 40 entries are 6 and 6, which average 6. So the median of the hours studied is 6.

■ The **mode** is the number that appears most often. Based on the data in Table 8, the mode of the number of hours studied is also 6 (8 students studied for 6 hours, so 6 appears 8 times in the list, more than any other number).

Graphical representations of the measures of central tendency may be presented in frequency polygons that take the form of curves, which may be normal or skewed.

■ Generally, if enough measures are taken of a variable and plotted as a frequency polygon, the result is a **normal curve** (bell-shaped curve), or **normal distribution** (Figure 25a). The curve is symmetrical, and the mean, median, and mode fall at the highest point on the curve.

■ **Skewed distributions** are asymmetrical, with most of the scores grouped toward one end. The mean, median, and mode fall at different points. Distributions may be skewed to the left (**negatively skewed**) (Figure 25b) or to the right (**positively skewed**) (Figure 25c).

Measures of Central Tendency

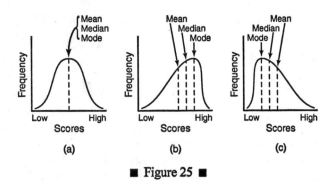

■ Figure 25 ■

- The frequency distribution termed **bimodal,** has two peaks, which represent two equal scores of highest frequency. In such a distribution, the mean and median may be at the same point or different points.

Measures of variation. **Variability** refers to the extent that scores differ from one another and from the mean. Widely used measures of variability are the range, variance, and standard deviation.

- The **range** describes the spread of scores in a distribution. It is calculated by subtracting the lowest from the highest score in the distribution. (In the example of hours of study, the range is $10 - 1 = 9$ hours.)

- The **variance** is a measure of variation from the mean of the squared deviation scores about the means of a distribution. Using the data from Table 8 as an example, the variance for the entire distribution is computed by

  —determining the mean of the distribution of data

$$\text{mean} = 5.6$$

  —subtracting the mean from each score to determine the **deviation score** for that item (Table 9, column 1)

  —squaring each deviation score (to eliminate minus signs) and multiplying it by the frequency of that score to account for the total number of scores (Table 9, column 2)

  —summing the results of the previous multiplication step (Table 9, last entry in column 2) to arrive at the total of all squared deviation scores and dividing by $(N-1)$ ($N =$ number of scores)

$$N - 1 = 40 - 1 = 39$$

$$\text{sum of each deviation score}^2 \times \text{frequency} = 177.60$$

$$\frac{177.60}{39} = 4.55 = \text{variance}$$

Some variance computations simply use N, but $(N-1)$ is considered to produce a more precise measurement. The variance gives one indication of how much the scores differ.

COMPUTATION OF DEVIATION SCORE, VARIANCE, AND STANDARD DEVIATION: HOURS STUDIED FOR AN EXAM	
Deviation Score (d) hours studied – mean = d	$d^2 \times$ **frequency**
$10 - 5.6 = 4.4$	$19.36 \times 1 = 19.36$
$9 - 5.6 = 3.4$	$11.56 \times 3 = 34.68$
$8 - 5.6 = 2.4$	$5.76 \times 4 = 23.04$
$7 - 5.6 = 1.4$	$1.96 \times 5 = 9.80$
$6 - 5.6 = 0.4$	$0.16 \times 8 = 1.28$
$5 - 5.6 = -0.6$	$0.36 \times 7 = 2.52$
$4 - 5.6 = -1.6$	$2.56 \times 5 = 12.80$
$3 - 5.6 = -2.6$	$6.76 \times 4 = 27.04$
$2 - 5.6 = -3.6$	$12.96 \times 2 = 25.92$
$1 - 5.6 = -4.6$	$21.16 \times 1 = 21.16$
	$N = 40 \quad \Sigma d^2 \times$ frequency $= 177.60$

$$\text{variance} = \frac{\text{sum of each deviation score}^2 \times \text{frequency}}{(N-1)}$$

$$= \frac{\Sigma d^2 \times \text{frequency}}{(N-1)}$$

$$= \frac{177.60}{39}$$

$$= 4.55$$

$$\text{standard deviation} = \text{square root of variance}$$

$$= \sqrt{4.55}$$

$$\cong 2.13$$

■ Table 9 ■

- The **standard deviation (SD)** is the square root of the variance.

  standard deviation $= \sqrt{\text{variance}}$

  standard deviation $= \sqrt{4.55} \cong 2.13$

Inferential Statistics

Inferential statistics involves mathematical procedures that allow psychologists to make inferences about collected data. For example, these procedures might be used to

- estimate the likelihood that the collected data occurred by chance (that is, to make probability predictions)

- to draw conclusions about a larger population from which samples were collected

The type of inferential statistical procedure used depends upon the type of measurement scale used as well as the distribution of the data. The procedures are usually used to test hypotheses and establish probability.

Sampling is the process of selecting cases to be tested from a larger population. For example, experimenters could not expect to measure the effects of a new therapeutic drug on every adult male in the population, so they would use a sample that is determined to be representative and unbiased. In inferential statistical procedures, the term **probability** refers to the likelihood that study results are statistically significant or that they are due to chance factors such as sampling errors. For example, if the significance level is determined to be .05, the researcher knows that the chances are only 5 out of 100, or 1 in 20, that the results were produced by chance factors alone.